Have Fun with AMERICAN HEROES

☆ ☆

Have Fun with
AMERICAN HEROES

Activities, Projects, and Fascinating Facts

David C. King

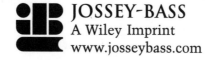

JOSSEY-BASS
A Wiley Imprint
www.josseybass.com

Published by Jossey-Bass
A Wiley Imprint
989 Market Street, San Francisco, CA 94103-1741

Illustration credits: © Bettman/Corbis, page 5 bottom; Cheryl Kirk Noll, page 60; Library of Congress, Prints and Photographs Division, page 10 top; Library of Congress, Prints and Photographs Division, Clifford Berryman Collection, page 53 bottom; Library Company of Philadelphia, page 17; Missouri Historical Society, page 20; all other illustrations, except for pages 6 top, 14 bottom, and 65 top © 2006 Len Shalansky.

Design and composition by Navta Associates, Inc.

Jossey-Bass books and products are available through most bookstores. To contact Jossey-Bass directly call our Customer Care Department within the U.S. at 800-956-7739, outside the U.S. at 317-572-3986, or fax 317-572-4002.

Jossey-Bass also publishes its books in a variety of electronic formats. Some content that appears in print may not be available in electronic books.

Library of Congress Cataloging-in-Publication Data:

King, David C., date.
  Have fun with American heroes : activities, projects, and fascinating facts / David C. King.
      p. cm.
  Includes index.
  ISBN-10 0-471-67904-6 (pbk.)
  ISBN-13 978-0-471-67904-2 (pbk.)
  1. Heroes—United States—Biography. 2. United States—Biography. I. Title.
  CT214.K56 2006
  920.073—dc22
                                                                2005008547

Printed in the United States of America

10 9 8 7 6 5 4 3 2 1

CONTENTS

INTRODUCTION

What makes a person a hero? When you hear the word *hero*, or *heroic*, what do you think of? Or who do you think of? For a lot of people, a hero is someone who displays great physical courage—a soldier leading troops into battle, or a firefighter carrying a child from a burning building. People like John F. Kennedy or General Douglas MacArthur come to mind. Of course there are many other ways of being a hero, including very quiet ways. Rosa Parks, for example, was a seamstress in Montgomery, Alabama, who became a hero when she refused to give up her seat on a segregated city bus.

In this book, you'll find that all kinds of people have become heroes—and often in very different ways. You'll discover, for instance, that George Washington had no desire to be a hero; he simply wanted to make his beloved Mount Vernon plantation the most successful farm in America. President Theodore Roosevelt, on the other hand, enjoyed being a hero, and he made the most of every moment in the spotlight. By contrast, Susan B. Anthony and Frederick Douglass were too busy fighting for justice and the rights of others to notice that they had become heroes.

Betsy Ross never even knew that she would be celebrated as the woman who worked secretly to sew the first United States flag. In fact, the story about her making the flag didn't emerge until a half-century later.

Our heroes have often been people who had the daring to explore in new directions. Daniel Boone and Lewis and Clark were among those who were determined to find out what lay beyond the mountains to the west. A century later, the Wright Brothers became heroes by pushing our frontiers into the sky. Daring aviators like Charles Lindbergh and Amelia Earhart then pushed the frontiers of flight further, paving the way for the heroes of space exploration like astronauts Neil Armstrong and Sally Ride.

Some men and women have performed heroically in their service to others or to the country. Abraham Lincoln guided the nation through the Civil War, for example, and Franklin D. Roosevelt provided hope and leadership through the country's greatest depression and World War II. On a less spectacular scale, reformer Jane Addams helped the poor in a Chicago slum, and Eleanor Roosevelt spoke out for those who had no spokesperson—the poor and the members of racial and ethnic minorities.

You'll encounter all of these people, and more, in the pages of this book. Reading about explorers like Lewis and Clark won't give you the skills needed for wilderness travel, but you can have fun measuring the height of a tree without climbing it. Reading about Ulysses S. Grant in the Civil War won't make you a battlefield expert, but you can work out the kinds of problems he dealt with in math and maps. You can also try some of the things these heroes enjoyed, like Benjamin Franklin's glass harmonica, one of the Wright Brothers' experiments, or Babe Ruth's ideas for the perfect baseball hot dog. Having fun while you learn about some of our country's greatest heroes is the main idea of this book.

Benjamin Franklin

Born *January 17, 1706, Boston, Massachusetts*
Died *April 17, 1790, Philadelphia, Pennsylvania*

Benjamin Franklin was the best-known American in the years before the Revolution—and also the most versatile. Among other pursuits, he was America's most successful printer, its first best-selling author, its most renowned scientist, an outstanding inventor, the most creative public official, and a diplomat who played a critical role in winning the nation's independence.

Franklin was born in Boston in 1706 and grew up there. He hated being a printer's apprentice for his brother and so he ran away, arriving in Philadelphia as a penniless seventeen-year-old. He became a printer and, at age twenty-four, owned a newspaper. He was successful enough to "retire" from business when he was forty-two to pursue his great interests—public affairs and science.

Among his many careers, he was a popular militia colonel in the 1750s; published a book called *Poor Richard's Almanac*, a best seller for twenty-five years; and, as a public official, gave Philadelphia its first paved streets, first fire company, and first regular police. Thanks to Franklin, Philadelphia was also the first city in the nation to have a lending library, a philosophical society, a public hospital, and a fire insurance company.

Franklin's activities for the country were equally creative and ambitious. As early as 1754, at a meeting of delegates from seven colonies, he proposed a union of all the colonies. But he was ahead of his time by about twenty years, and no colony approved it. He served as postmaster for the colonies, and he spent the better part of twenty years representing several colonies in England. He was a delegate to the Second Continental Congress, served on the committee chosen to help write the Declaration of Independence, and later, in his eighties, served at the Constitutional Convention. As minister to France, from 1776 through 1783, he engineered an alliance with France that made victory in the Revolutionary War possible.

In writing the Declaration of Independence, Franklin and the other delegates were putting their lives on the line because, from the British viewpoint, they were all guilty of treason. Franklin famously summed up the delegates' position by declaring that "We must now all hang together or, most assuredly, we shall all hang separately."

All Knowledge Is Useful

Franklin never stopped learning, and he believed that all knowledge has value. Once, while watching a hot air balloon in Paris, a friend asked what possible use this new toy could have. Franklin's reply: "Of what use is a newborn baby?"

Always Joking

Franklin was famous for his sense of humor. It was said that although he was on the committee to help write the Declaration of Independence, the Congress did not want him actually to write it because they were afraid he might hide a joke in it.

3

© 2006 by John Wiley & Sons, Inc.

As a scientist, his famous experiment with a kite and a key in a lightning storm led to his invention of the lightning rod—a device that practically eliminated a major cause of fires in his day. He invented the Franklin stove, which was a great improvement in home heating. And when he was in his eighties, his own failing eyesight led to his invention of bifocal eyeglasses. As you would expect, he never really retired. When he died in 1790, his funeral was the occasion for the largest public gathering ever seen in the nation up to that time.

The Glass Harmonica

In 1761, Franklin invented a musical instrument called an *armonica*, using bowls of water in a complex contraption to produce different notes. Several famous composers, including Mozart and Beethoven, wrote pieces for it. Franklin had earlier created a simpler invention—the glass harmonica. Try it yourself.

Things You'll Need

8 identical glasses, as tall and as thin as possible (use only with your parents' permission!)

large tray (a countertop will do)

large pitcher of water

2 pencils, or stir sticks, or chopsticks

towel, paper towels, or a sponge (for cleanup, if needed)

1 Arrange the glasses in a row. Fill the glass on the left about ¾ full of water. Moisten the rim and tap it gently with a stir stick. You should get a low tone.

2 Fill the second glass with a little less water, the third with still less water, and so on until all eight have some water. Experiment with the water levels and you'll be able to produce the 8-note scale—do, re, mi, fa, so, la, ti, do.

3 Once you have the scale, you can try playing tunes—or even composing your own.

Write an Acrostic

Franklin loved playing with words and he was also fond of bits of wisdom. Consequently, he was delighted when an uncle showed him how to write simple verses called *acrostics*. Acrostics are poems in which the first letter of each line spells out a word or a name. Try writing an acrostic using your name or the name Benjamin Franklin. Here is a sample, in Ben's words:

Be ever truthful in all things.
Even when temptation
    troubles you, do
    not weaken.
Never take more than
    you need and you
    will never want.

In Their Own WORDS

A slip of the Foot you may soon recover, But a slip of the Tongue you may never get over.

GEORGE WASHINGTON

Born *February 22, 1732, Westmoreland County, Virginia*
Died *December 14, 1799, Mount Vernon, Virginia*

George Washington never wanted to be the "father of his country." What he really wanted was to be a farmer and to make his estate, Mount Vernon, a model of modern farming. But his country kept needing him, and he managed only occasional visits to his home.

Washington had been born into Virginia's wealthy class—the families who owned the huge farms called *plantations* and who also held the important positions in government and in the colony's military force, the *militia*. Washington made the most of his privileged position and by age twenty-three was in command of Virginia's militia. He married Martha Custis, a widow, and adopted her two children.

He was a commanding figure, the kind of man who seems born to lead. He had a powerful 6'2" frame, was fearless in battle, and inspired his men with his courage and determination. He displayed his great courage early in the French and Indian War (1756–1763). At one time, in avoiding an ambush, he wrote, "I luckily escaped without a wound, though I had four bullets through my coat, and two horses shot under me."

When the American Revolution began in April 1775, the Continental Congress chose Washington to create and command a Continental Army. For the next six years, he managed to keep an army in the field by shrewd tactics and by avoiding pitched battles against the British Army, the world's mightiest military force. One of his most courageous moves was leading his troops across the ice-clogged Delaware River on Christmas night, 1776, to win stunning victories at Trenton and Princeton. In 1781, another bold move by Washington led the army to the final American victory at the battle of Yorktown.

After a brief retirement at Mount Vernon, he presided over the Constitutional Convention in 1787 and then was the unanimous choice to be the first president of the United States of America. His two terms in that office provided the stability needed to launch America's great experiment in democracy.

How to Stop Invading Armies

During the Constitutional Convention, an amendment was proposed to limit the nation's army to five thousand men. Washington said that was fine with him—as long as invading armies were told they could not use more than three thousand men.

He was finally able to retire in 1797, but illness robbed him of a long retirement and he died in 1799. In a eulogy, one of his generals summed up Washington with three famous phrases, saying that Washington was "First in war, first in peace, and first in the hearts of his countrymen!"

Presidential Dentures

Washington needed false teeth for much of his adult life. They usually were painful, including the first pair, which was made from hippopotamus ivory. Later sets, made of wood, were not much better. Some people say that Washington has such a dour expression in portraits because his teeth hurt.

Design a Medal for Heroism

Whenever someone performed a heroic act during the American Revolution, the Continental Congress ordered the creation of a special medal to honor the hero. The figures to the right show the front and back of the first medal ordered by Congress, which honored Washington for forcing the British to evacuate Boston in 1776. Design a coin to honor Washington for the crossing of the Delaware to attack Trenton. Design both sides on a circular piece of cardboard.

Things You'll Need

grated rind of 1 large lemon
3 tablespoons lemon juice
1 cup sugar
mixing bowl
mixing spoon
2 cups light cream
⅛ teaspoon salt
2 ice cube trays
MAKES 1½ PINTS

Mount Vernon Lemon Ice Cream

Washington had a great love of ice cream, which was developed in Italy in the 1760s. (The French also claim credit, and one eighteenth-century author said Washington was the father of the popular dessert). Washington once ran up a bill of several hundred dollars with a New York ice cream merchant for a single summer. The recipe here, attributed to Washington, is for an early way to make ice cream, before the invention of the hand-cranked ice cream freezer. (Most plantations and farms had access to ice-houses or ice caves where ice was stored in large blocks.)

1 Mix the rind, juice, and sugar together in a medium-size mixing bowl, and slowly stir in the cream and salt.

2 Stir well.

3 Pour into ice cube trays (remove the dividers) and freeze.

4 When the outer edges are firm, after about one hour, remove from the freezer and stir well with a wooden spoon; then cover and freeze. (Times will vary.)

A Man of Few Words

Washington's second inaugural address was only 133 words long. He delivered it in two minutes!

In Their Own WORDS

The power of the Constitution will always be in the people.

Daniel Boone

Born *November 2, 1734, Reading, Pennsylvania*
Died *September 26, 1820, St. Charles County, Missouri*

Daniel Boone was the greatest frontiersman in the history of early America. He was a courageous and resourceful trailblazer who played a leading role in opening the lands west of the Appalachians to settlers. He became such a legend in his own lifetime that it is sometimes difficult to separate the facts of his life from the myths.

Boone was born near present-day Reading, Pennsylvania, but his family moved to the frontier of North Carolina when he was in his teens. Although he had no formal schooling, he did learn to read and write. By age twelve, he was a skilled hunter and trapper and an expert marksman.

From the mid-1760s on, his name became associated with the land known as "Kentucke." Between 1767 and 1775, he made four long trips into that wilderness to the west and became captivated by its rugged beauty. "We found everywhere abundance of wild beasts of all sorts," he wrote. "The buffalo were more frequent than I have seen cattle in the settlements."

Boone and his companions were in constant danger, and several, including his son, were tortured and killed by warriors of the Shawnee and other tribes. Encouraged by the British, the Native American tribes fought ferociously to drive out the white intruders. However, nothing weakened Boone's love of the land. "I returned to my family," he wrote in 1769, "with a determination to bring them as soon as possible to live in Kentucke, which I esteemed a second paradise, at the risk of my life and fortune."

In 1775, Boone and twenty-eight woodsmen blazed a trail called the Wilderness Road through the Cumberland Gap; it became the major route from Virginia into the West. A few months later, he brought his wife, Rebecca, and their daughter, Jemima, as well as a party of settlers, to establish Boonesboro, the first pioneer settlement in Kentucky. In 1778, Boone himself was captured by Shawnee warriors and held for five months. He managed to escape in time to warn Boonesboro of an attack by warriors of several tribes and British troops. The settlers managed to survive a ten-day assault.

Boone's reputation took on mythical proportions after the publication of a book by John Filson in 1784—*The Discovery, Settlement, and Present State of Kentucky*. The book contained what was claimed to be Boone's autobiography. While the book was based on his actual journals, Filson changed some of Boone's words into the flowery phrases of a real estate promoter.

In spite of his heroism, Boone did not prosper. Some Kentuckians, envious of his fame, claimed that he had really been a spy for the British. In addition,

Boone's Literary Fame

John Filson's book was widely read in Europe and America, and Boone's heroic life story became a model for several writers, such as James Fenimore Cooper, who wrote *The Last of the Mohicans*.

A Resourceful Daughter

In 1777, Boone's daughter and two friends were kidnapped by Shawnee warriors. The girls managed to break twigs and tear off bits of clothing in order to leave a trail. Boone followed the trail for three days and rescued them.

his claim to ten thousand acres of land was denied when Kentucky became a state. Feeling rejected by the state he had helped to create, Boone moved to present-day Missouri in 1799 and remained there until his death in 1820.

★ Cook a Batch of Sappawn

Hunters and trappers like Daniel Boone kept cornmeal in their packs for a quick meal to go with dried or salted meat. The Boone family would have used a cornmeal mush that was called *sappawn* in Pennsylvania and *hasty pudding* in coastal Virginia. Your sappawn will make a tasty and healthy breakfast cereal.

1 Measure the water, cornmeal, and salt into the saucepan.

2 Have your adult helper help you cook the mixture over medium heat, stirring often. When the sappawn begins to bubble and steam rises, reduce the heat to low and cook for at least 12 minutes, stirring almost constantly. (Note: If you can do it, continue cooking and stirring for up to 15 minutes more. This is how the pioneers did it. Longer cooking improves the flavor.)

3 Let the sappawn cool for a few minutes. Serve in cereal bowls while still warm, and stir in raisins, maple syrup, or brown sugar. Most kids like to pour on milk.

★ Things You'll Need

measuring cup and spoon
medium saucepan
2 cups water
⅓ cup yellow cornmeal
½ teaspoon salt
wooden mixing spoon
timer or clock
serving bowls and spoons
raisins, maple syrup, or
  brown sugar
milk (optional)
adult helper
MAKES 4 SERVINGS

★ Make a Compass

If Boone became lost, he could use the sun or the stars to find his way. If he could determine one compass direction, usually north, he knew that west would be to the left, east to the right, and south directly opposite north.

When he was surveying land he planned to claim or purchase, he needed a compass. Most colonists either had a compass or knew how to make a simple one using the following directions.

1 Push the nail through the center of the cork. The nail should stick out from both ends of the cork.

2 Brush the nail across the magnet ten or twelve times, always brushing in the same direction. This magnetizes the nail.

3 Place the cork in the pan and watch the cork slowly turn. The nail will line itself up with the magnetic North pole. If you move the bowl or turn it, your compass will automatically find the pole again.

★ Things You'll Need

1½- to 2-inch nail
cork from a bottle
magnet (a bar magnet, if
  possible, available at
  hardware stores)
small pan of water (glass or
  plastic—not metal)

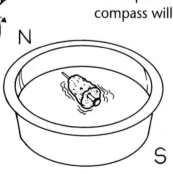

In Their Own WORDS

Thus situated, many hundred miles from our families, in the howling wilderness, I believe few would have equally enjoyed the happiness we experienced.

Paul Revere

Born *January 1, 1735, Boston, Massachusetts*
Died *May 10, 1818, Boston, Massachusetts*

Paul Revere is best known as the patriot on horseback who delivered a warning to the towns west of Boston that British troops were on the way. That warning, on the night of April 18, 1775, enabled the volunteer soldiers—the Minutemen—to be ready to take on the British in the first battles of the American Revolution. At the time, however, no one paid a lot of attention to Revere's "midnight ride." It was not until eighty years later, when America's favorite poet, Henry Wadsworth Longfellow, wrote a stirring poem about it, that the ride took on mythical proportions. Even without the ride and without Longfellow's poetic intervention, Revere was one of the great figures in the struggle for independence.

Revere grew up in Boston, attended local schools, and learned his father's trade of silversmithing. He was nineteen when his father died and he took over the business. He was married by age twenty-two and eventually had eight children, so he had to keep working hard. By 1765, the shop was becoming famous for its outstanding silver and pewter work. Many of his pewter and silver pieces, such as trays, bowls, and coffee services, are museum pieces today, and they brought increasingly high prices in the late 1700s.

As trouble with England developed in the mid-1760s, Revere became active in local politics. He became an *express* (a mounted messenger) for the patriots and continued in that role for several years, gaining fame for his swift delivery of messages to New York and Philadelphia.

Early in 1775, the patriots learned that the British were planning a raid to seize patriot weapons and to arrest two key leaders, Samuel Adams and John Hancock. With a band of spies and messengers called the "mechanics," Revere kept a close watch on the British in Boston. On the night of April 18, 1775, Revere and John Dawes alerted more than twenty towns in time for their militia to prepare.

During the Revolution, Revere served in the military for a time, produced gunpowder, and made cannons for the patriot cause. He also designed and printed the first Continental currency. After the war, he returned to his profitable trades. At age sixty-five he learned to roll copper and established the first industry for covering the hulls of wooden ships, including the *Constitution*, with copper sheathing for protection. He remained active nearly until his death at age eighty-three.

Military Pride

Revere's military adventures were not great successes, but he was tremendously proud of having served in the army; so proud, in fact, that he wore a uniform every day until his death nearly forty years after the war.

Unfinished Journey

Paul Revere and John Dawes were supposed to ride to Lexington and Concord, but neither made it all the way. They were stopped by British officers outside Lexington. Dawes got away and headed home; Revere was released but stayed in Lexington to help Adams and Hancock. A young doctor, Samuel Prescott, who had joined them on his way home from his fiancée's house, escaped the British and carried the warning to Concord.

☆ ☆

Revere and the Boston Massacre

In 1770, Revere created a "broadside" (a one-page news sheet) giving his version of an unintended shooting the patriots called the "Boston Massacre." Revere purposely made his drawing inaccurate. For example, he has the British soldiers shooting at point-blank range, rather than at a distance of 15 to 20 feet. The colonists appear unarmed and well-dressed, although it was really a rowdy bunch who were hurling rocks and snowballs at the outnumbered soldiers. These exaggerations helped make the broadside one of the most effective propaganda pieces of the Revolution.

☆ ☆

The Spy's Secret Code

Spying was common by both sides during the American Revolution, and people used a variety of secret codes to foil the enemy. During the tense days of 1774–1776, Revere and his "mechanics" knew that someone was reporting their movements to British headquarters in Boston. (At the same time, someone was reporting British plans to the patriots.) Finally, a messenger became suspicious of a letter written by a respected American physician, Dr. Benjamin Church. When the letter was opened, the writing looked like this:

GSV IVTRNVMG DROO NZIXS ZG WZDM

Can you decipher the doctor's code?

Actually, this code is one of the oldest, dating back some 2,500 years, and also one of the easiest to decipher. The key is simple: it's a reverse alphabet, so that ZYX = ABC. Write out the alphabet from A to Z; underneath it, write the reverse, with A under Z, B under Y, and so on. Now you can break the doctor's secret code and use it to exchange messages with a friend. The answer appears at the back of the book.

What Revere Didn't Say

We often read that Paul Revere rode through sleeping villages shouting "The British are coming! The British are coming!" He probably never said that, because the colonists still considered themselves British citizens. It's more likely he would have shouted "The regulars are coming!" or "The redcoats are coming!"

In Their Own
WORDS

Noise! You'll have noise enough before long. The regulars are coming out!

Create a Broadside

Paul Revere's broadside of the Boston Massacre was drawn to make the British troops look like murderers, and it proved to be very effective. Modern editorial cartoonists employ the same technique of exaggeration. Try creating a broadside to present your ideas about an important event. The event can be something historical or current, like a social or environmental matter you feel strongly about, or an unfair practice in sports or business that you feel should be corrected. Use words as well as a picture.

PATRICK HENRY

Born *May 29, 1736, Hanover County, Virginia*
Died *June 6, 1799, Charlotte County, Virginia*

There was not much in the early life of Patrick Henry to suggest his future greatness. He was born on the frontier of Virginia and educated at home. He married Sarah Shelton when he was eighteen while he was still searching for a career. He tried farming but failed, and then went broke twice as a storekeeper. Finally, in his mid-twenties, he taught himself law and enjoyed almost instant success as a lawyer. In his first three years, he argued 1,185 cases, winning most. With a powerful speaking voice and the dramatic skills of an actor, he quickly became known as the most persuasive orator in America.

Henry was a member of the House of Burgesses (Virginia's legislature) when the trouble began between the colonies and Great Britain. In 1763, he led Virginia's protest against the hated Stamp Act. In a fiery speech denouncing King George III, he declared, "If this be treason, make the most of it!"

Over the next decade, Henry became a leader of the patriot cause. In March 1775, he delivered his most famous speech when he urged Virginia to join the New England colonies in fighting for their rights. With dramatic gestures, he declared, "I know not what course others may take, but as for me, give me liberty or give me death!" George Washington and Thomas Jefferson were among those who sat in stunned silence as Henry finished his dramatic delivery.

Henry remained an effective leader throughout the Revolution. He served in both the First and Second Continental Congresses, helped write a state constitution for Virginia, and served as the state's first governor. Once independence was won, however, he stunned his fellow patriots by refusing to be a delegate to the Constitutional Convention in 1787 and then vigorously opposing the new Constitution. Henry believed that a strong central government would trample on the liberties of the people and the states. His opposition had a powerful impact: it was a major reason for adding a Bill of Rights to the Constitution— ten amendments guaranteeing the rights of the people and the states.

The Stamp Act

The Stamp Act of 1763 was Great Britain's first attempt to place a tax directly on the people. Colonists had to pay for a stamp on every paper item, even newspapers and playing cards. The vigorous protests soon led Parliament to cancel the tax.

In the late 1790s, Henry again puzzled people by becoming a firm supporter of the Constitution and the government. President George Washington offered him several major posts, including secretary of state and chief justice of the Supreme Court, but declining health forced him to refuse the appointments. Elected to serve in the Virginia legislature again in 1799, Henry agreed, but he died before he could take the post.

★ Build a Word

Figure out the clues to find the six words and write your answers in the spaces. One is done for you. Unscramble the letters in the squares to find a word that describes Patrick Henry.

1 Patrick Henry said to make the most of it.

1 [T] R E A S O N

2 He wanted, not death but . . .

2 _ _ _ _ _ ☐ _ _

3 He first gained fame as one.

3 _ _ _ _ _ ☐

4 He served in both the first and second . . .

4 _ ☐ _ _ _ _ _ _ _

5 What he asked for if he couldn't have number 2.

5 _ _ ☐ _ _

6 He insisted this be added to the Constitution.

6 _ _ _ _ ☐ _ _ _ _ _ _

7 Patrick Henry was a great one.

7 ☐☐☐☐☐☐

Answers appear at the back of the book.

★ The Kids' Bill of Rights

Even before Thomas Jefferson wrote the Declaration of Independence, Patrick Henry had argued that people had certain natural, God-given rights that must be protected. He insisted on a Bill of Rights being added to the Constitution in order to protect those rights from the government.

What about the rights of kids? What rights do you think are important to yourself and other kids, such as the right to privacy, or the right to a safe environment, or the right to eat the foods you choose?

Make a poster stating your bill of rights for kids. Work with a friend, using a large piece of construction paper or posterboard, pencils, crayons or felt-tip pens, and maybe something to decorate the document, like artwork and stickers or glitter. The rights can be stated in full sentences or in slogan-like phrases. You can also use library resources to find what kinds of rights are mentioned in the United Nations Convention on the Rights of the Child.

In Their Own WORDS

Gentlemen may cry, peace, peace, but there is no peace. The war is actually begun! The next gale that sweeps from the north will bring to our ears the clash of resounding arms!

THOMAS ★★★★★★★★★★★★★★★★★★★★★★★★★★★★★★★★
JEFFERSON
★★★★★★★★★★★★★★★★★★★★★★★★★★★★★★★★★★★★★★

Born *April 11, 1743, Albemarle County, Virginia*
Died *July 4, 1826, Charlottesville, Virginia*

One of the most remarkable things about Thomas Jefferson was his versatility. In fact, it's hard to believe that one person could excel in so many different roles—president, diplomat, historian, writer, architect, scientist, farmer, inventor, musician, and language scholar. And still, even after his retirement from the presidency at age sixty-three, he found time to write more than a thousand letters every year.

As a member of Virginia's wealthy plantation class, it was natural for Jefferson to pursue a career in law and government. But he also became an outstanding scholar who wrote on a variety of subjects, including history, political science, natural science, and farming, winning acclaim throughout Europe as well as America.

As a delegate to the Continental Congress in the mid-1770s, Jefferson quickly became known for his writing skills and, in 1776, became the major author of the Declaration of Independence, one of the cornerstones of American democracy. Five years later, while governor of Virginia, he penned the Virginia Statute of Religious Freedom, a document that made the United States the world's leader in religious freedom. As president, he guided the nation through the Louisiana Purchase, which more than doubled the country's land area.

July 4, 1826—A Most Special Day

Both John Adams, the nation's second president, and Jefferson, the third, lived long lives. Adams had also been with Jefferson on the committee to draft the Declaration of Independence. After Jefferson retired from the presidency, the two carried on an extensive correspondence. In one of history's most amazing coincidences, Adams and Jefferson both died on July 4, 1826—the fiftieth anniversary of the signing of the Declaration of Independence.

☆☆☆☆☆☆☆☆☆☆☆

Inventor and Innovator

Jefferson invented folding chairs and folding doors, the first dumbwaiter in America, and the best plow in use until 1830. He also introduced new ideas and products from Europe, including ice cream, macaroni (and a machine to make it), and the recipe for Parmesan cheese. He also receives credit for creating the dishes baked Alaska and chicken à la king, a favorite of George Washington's.

☆☆☆☆☆☆☆☆☆☆☆

As an architect, Jefferson had a lasting impact on American styles through the design of his famous home, Monticello. He also designed the state capitol at Richmond and the buildings for the University of Virginia.

After retiring from his two terms as president in 1809, he devoted himself to Monticello and to planning the University of Virginia, while continuing his work in natural science, gardening, agriculture, and the study of Indian languages.

★ Using Secret Codes

Secret codes have been used in military and diplomatic affairs for more than two thousand years. Thomas Jefferson was skilled at deciphering codes and creating them. He thought the codes would be useful for sending sensitive information to diplomats serving in other countries. He developed one of the most complicated codes, which used thirty-six wooden wheels on an iron rod, with each wheel containing a scrambled alphabet. The U.S. Navy used the "Jefferson Cipher" for a time in the early 1900s. Not until the age of computers did anyone establish so elaborate a code system as Jefferson's.

Here is one of the easiest codes to use. It's been around since about 500 B.C.E. In the grid shown here, identify and use letters by looking at the *row* first, then at the *column*. The letter R, for example, would be 43 (because it's in the fourth row and the third column). The word HERO would be 23-15-43-35. Use the checkerboard grid to decipher this message:

columns

	1	2	3	4	5
1	A	B	C	D	E
2	F	G	H	I	J
3	K	L	M	N	O
4	P	Q	R	S	T
5	U	V	W	X	Y/z

rows

43-15-11-14   53-24-45-23   13-11-43-15

The answer appears at the back of the book.
Now work with a friend to exchange secret messages.

Make a Terrarium

Gardening, including farming, was Jefferson's great passion. For more than sixty years he kept a gardening journal. He corresponded with botanists and gardeners all over the world and introduced new plants to Virginia, including garlic and oranges as well as various flowers. "The greatest service that can be rendered any country," he wrote, "is to add a useful plant to its culture." Indoors he kept a *terrarium*, also known at the time as a "glass garden," so that he could study different kinds of soil, moisture levels, and plant varieties all year round.

A terrarium has long been a popular way to create an indoor garden that requires very little care. It can also be a great home for a salamander or a small turtle.

Here's a chance to model Jefferson's curiosity about nature along with his skill at making things.

1 Make sure the jar is clean. Spread the pebbles or stones on the bottom.

2 Spoon (or shovel) the soil on top of the stones.

3 Place your plants in the soil, packing a little soil around them.

4 Arrange larger stones, bark, and wood scraps around the plantings to make an attractive arrangement.

5 Use the hammer and nail to make six or eight holes in the jar lid, from the top down. You can file down the jagged edges or cover them with adhesive tape.

6 Fill the spray bottle with water and give your terrarium a good misting. Put on the lid and place the jar in a location with *partial* sun. Water vapor will form on the sides, usually in direct sunlight. When the sides remain dry, it's time to add more spray.

Things You'll Need

large glass or plastic jar, with a large mouth and a lid (the kind used for bulk foods in supermarkets is perfect), or an old aquarium with a cover.

2 or 3 handfuls of small stones or pebbles

clean soil (or potting soil)—enough for a 3-inch to 4-inch layer in the bottom of the jar

old mixing spoon or child's sand shovel

some small plants, such as moss, ferns, ivy

a few pieces of wood bark or small scraps, and a larger stone or two

large nail and hammer

adhesive tape or metal file

spray bottle

In Their Own WORDS

Nature intended me for the tranquil pursuits of science, by rendering them my supreme delight.

15

Betsy ★ Ross

Born *January 1, 1752, Philadelphia, Pennsylvania*
Died *January 30, 1836, Philadelphia, Pennsylvania*

We all know that Betsy Ross made the first United States flag, or at least we *think* she did. Many historians question the story because there is no real evidence to prove it. One bit of evidence in favor of the story is that Betsy placed an order for a large amount of flag cloth in June 1776. Whether or not she did sew and help design the first flag, her story is an interesting one.

Elizabeth (Betsy) Griscom was born in Philadelphia in 1752. Her parents were Quakers, a religious sect that believes in nonviolence. The Quakers were also unusual for the time because they believed in educating their daughters as well as their sons, and teaching them a trade. Betsy became an upholstery apprentice and worked on a wide variety of sewing projects.

When she was twenty-one, Betsy eloped with John Ross and they started their own upholstery business. Her family—and the Quaker community—disowned her for marrying a non-Quaker. Betsy retaliated by starting her own, more liberal, Quaker group. John, a militiaman, was killed on duty in January 1776, not long after their marriage.

Betsy continued the family business and was doing well when her late husband's uncle, George Ross, a leading patriot, visited her in June 1776 with two other men, Robert Morris and General George Washington. They explained their mission: the thirteen colonies were about to declare their independence from Great Britain. Would Mrs. Ross make a flag for the new nation? She agreed. Some accounts say that Washington had a sketch of the flag, while other versions say that Ross sketched it. This first American flag included the stars and stripes, but instead of fifty stars there were thirteen, one for each state, arranged in a circle. Apparently Betsy Ross completed the project secretly, since secrecy would have been essential; if discovered, she could have been arrested and tried for treason.

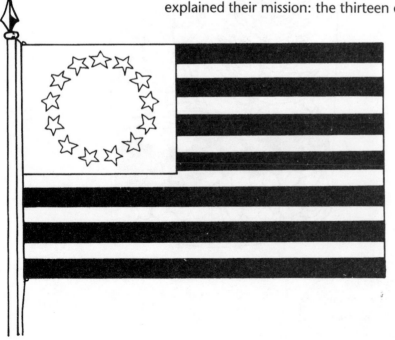

The Imaginary Portrait

There is no portrait of the real Betsy Ross. The most famous painting of her, titled "Birth of our Nation's Flag," was based on pictures of other family members.

Betsy Ross was a good businesswoman, and her shop prospered for many years. She did not have such good luck with husbands, however. About eighteen months after John Ross was killed, she married Joseph Ashburn, a ship's captain. His ship was captured by the British, and he died in a British prison in 1782. John Claypoole, who had known Ashburn in prison, came to Philadelphia to see Betsy in 1783. They fell in love and were married. She also outlived her third husband. Betsy kept the upholstery business going until about 1830, then turned it over to her daughter. She died at the age of eighty-four.

The "Fighting Quakers"

The new Quaker group started by Betsy Ross called themselves "Free Quakers." The roughly two hundred members abandoned traditional Quaker nonviolence in order to support the patriot cause. New Englanders called them the "Fighting Quakers."

Mysteries about the Flag

Most historians believe that the design of the flag was based on a drawing by Francis Hopkinson, a New Jersey delegate to the Continental Congress, which approved the stars-and-stripes design on June 14, 1777. No one knows when Ross might have finished the flag, nor do we know where and when it was first flown. It could have been in use some months before Congress approved it.

Things You'll Need

½ gallon vanilla ice cream

shallow rectangular cake pan about 13 by 9 inches

measuring cup

1 cup white cake frosting

blue and red food coloring

table knife

teaspoon

ruler

13 white yogurt-covered raisins

MAKES 4–6 SERVINGS

An Ice Cream Flag

Here's a cool way to honor the Betsy Ross flag. You can also celebrate Flag Day (June 14) or July 4.

1 Let the ice cream soften a little so you can spread it flat to cover the bottom of the cake pan. Then put it in the freezer until the ice cream is hard.

2 Spoon about half the frosting into the measuring cup. Add a little blue food coloring and stir well with a spoon. Continue stirring and adding food coloring until you have a deep blue color. If the frosting becomes stiff, add a little water.

3 Remove the ice cream from the freezer. Use a table knife to spread the blue frosting in a rectangle in the upper left corner of the ice cream. It should measure about 4 inches tall and 5 inches wide.

4 Wash the measuring cup and repeat step 2 using the red food coloring.

5 With the knife and spoon, make a narrow strip of red across the top of the ice cream flag, starting at the right-hand edge of the blue rectangle.

6 Make a second red stripe below the first, leaving a white space in between. To fit seven red stripes and six white ones, each stripe should be about $^{11}/_{16}$ inches wide. That's pretty delicate measuring, so you can adjust it by making fewer stripes and keeping them as straight as you can.

7 Arrange thirteen yogurt-covered raisins in a circle on the blue field. Serve your ice cream flag proudly. If your celebration is on July 4, sing "Happy Birthday" to the United States.

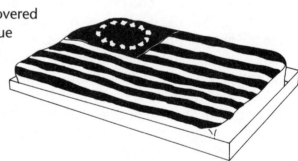

Design a Flag

With white paper, pencil, and crayons or colored pencils, design a flag for something special—your city, town, or school, for example, or a Native American tribe, or an event like Earth Day. Sketch the design first. When you're satisfied with your flag design, draw it on a sheet of white paper and color it.

In Their Own WORDS *I will try it!*

LEWIS and CLARK

MERIWETHER LEWIS
   Born *August 18, 1774, Albemarle County, Virginia*
   Died *October 11, 1809, Nashville, Tennessee*

WILLIAM CLARK
   Born *August 1, 1770, Caroline County, Virginia*
   Died *September 1, 1838, St. Louis, Missouri*

The names Lewis and Clark have remained inseparable since their extraordinary expedition across the uncharted West of North America from 1804 to 1806. They were gone for twenty-eight months, so long that many people gave them up for lost. They encountered more than fifty Native American tribes, but they had only one (brief) armed clash and lost only one man (who died from appendicitis). They brought back a treasure trove of useful information, and, perhaps most important, they expanded people's thinking, enabling them to see the Far West as theirs to explore and settle.

The expedition was the brainchild of President Thomas Jefferson, who set the wheels in motion even before several lucky breaks led France to sell the vast area of the Louisiana Territory to the United States for a mere $23 million in 1803. Jefferson asked Meriwether Lewis, his neighbor and personal secretary, to lead the expedition. Lewis, who had served on the frontier with the U.S. Army, asked another former officer, William Clark, to be co-captain of what they called the Corps of Discovery.

The expedition of nearly fifty men pushed off from St. Louis on May 14, 1804, heading up the Missouri River in two large canoes and a 55-foot keelboat. By November, they were in the territory of friendly Mandan Indians and wintered over near one of the Mandan villages. The following April, with seventeen-year-old Sacagawea and her husband, Toussaint Charbonneau, as guides, they began probing for a waterway that might carry them all the way to the Pacific Coast. They encountered enormous hardships, largely because so little was known of the geography. For example, they thought that the Rocky Mountains formed a single barrier, but found

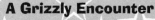
A Grizzly Encounter

Six members of the Corps of Discovery were hunting when they encountered what they called "a very large brown bear"—a grizzly. Four of the men fired at the huge bear, two of the shots passing through the bear's lungs. This only led the animal to charge. The other two hunters got off shots that struck the grizzly but only slowed him a little. Running while reloading and shooting, the men made it to a river and plunged in, with the bear close behind. Several more shots were fired before they finally killed the bear. In examining the bear, they found that eight shots had gone completely through him. Nothing wrong with their aim!

instead that they had to cross several parallel ranges. They also thought that all but a very short distance to the coast could be covered by water, only to learn that there was much difficult travel that had to be made on horseback and on foot. That Sacagawea was able to obtain horses from her Shoshone tribe was a vital factor in the expedition's survival and success.

In spite of the hardships, including near-starvation when they ran out of food in the snow-clogged mountain passes, they reached the mighty Columbia River, hastily built some dugout canoes, and rode them to the Pacific Ocean, reaching the coast in November 1805. They wintered near present-day Astoria, Oregon, and began the return journey overland in March 1806. Their arrival in St. Louis in September, after a journey of nearly eight thousand miles, touched off a nationwide celebration.

Meriwether Lewis was later named governor of the new Louisiana Territory. In 1809, he headed back to Washington, but on the way he died of a gunshot wound under mysterious circumstances, most likely a suicide. William Clark was placed in charge of the militia and of Indian affairs. In 1813, he became governor of the new Missouri Territory. He continued to work for peace with the Native American tribes until his death in 1838.

© 2006 by John Wiley & Sons, Inc.

Lewis's Wounds

Lewis and two other men, on a side exploration, experienced the one violent encounter with Native Americans, and were forced to shoot their way out of trouble. Captain Lewis escaped without a scratch, but a few days later he was shot—he received a load of buckshot when one of the men mistook his buckskin-clad rear end for an elk. The wounds were not serious, except perhaps to his pride.

☆☆☆☆☆☆☆☆☆☆☆☆☆☆☆☆☆☆☆☆☆☆☆☆☆☆

Writing Assignments

President Jefferson wanted every member of the expedition who could read and write to keep a journal. In addition, for insurance, he suggested that an official record be kept on waterproof birch bark. The journals provided a treasure of information about the West and also whetted Americans' appetites to explore further.

☆☆☆☆☆☆☆☆☆☆☆☆☆☆☆☆☆☆☆☆☆☆☆☆☆☆

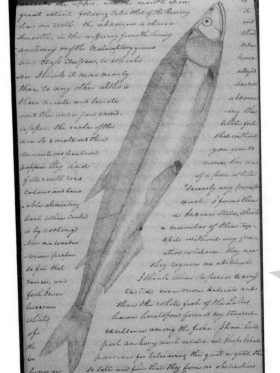

An Illustrated Journal

Neither Lewis nor Clark had any training in art, and yet they boldly filled their journals with sketches and very careful drawings, as well as with words. Try keeping a journal on a trip or on a hike. Include sketches of things that interest you, like buildings, wildlife, and people.

Measuring Tree Height

In response to President Jefferson's instructions, Lewis and Clark tried to be as accurate and precise as possible in reporting what they saw. When they encountered gigantic trees near the Pacific Coast, for example, they had to figure out a way to describe the height of those great trees. One method they could use was commonly employed by shipbuilders to measure trees for masts. You can try this yourself.

tape measure
the tree you want to measure
helper
straight pole or stick

1 Use the tape measure to measure 60 feet from the base of the tree. Have your helper hold the pole at the 60-foot mark. He or she should keep the pole straight.

2 Measure an additional 6 feet from the tree, starting at the pole.

3 Lie down with your head at the 6-foot mark and your feet pointing toward the pole and the tree, as shown in the drawing. Your head will be 6 feet from the pole and 66 feet from the tree.

4 Keep your head as close to the ground as possible and look past the pole to the top of the tree. You will see the top of the tree somewhere along the pole. Have your helper move his or her hand up or down the pole to mark the point on the pole where you see the top of the tree.

5 Now measure the distance on the pole from the ground to your helper's hand. Multiply that distance by 11 to get the tree's height. Example: If your helper's hand is 34 inches from the ground, the tree is 374 inches tall, or a little more than 31 feet.

How it works: You created a right-angle triangle and you know one side measures 66 feet. Your sighting enables you to measure the other two sides.

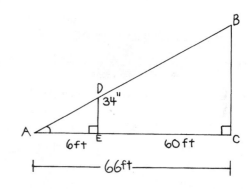

In Their Own
WORDS

In obedience to our orders, we have penetrated the continent of North America to the Pacific Ocean.

21

Sacagawea

Born ca. 1787, western Montana or eastern Idaho
Died December 20, 1812?, Omaha, Nebraska

Sacagawea was only about seventeen years old when she walked into the pages of history with the Lewis and Clark Expedition of 1804–1806. Little is known about her life either before or after that historic event. The expedition leaders, Meriwether Lewis and William Clark, were more interested at the beginning in hiring her husband, a French Canadian fur trader named Toussaint Charbonneau, to be their interpreter and guide. They agreed to have Sacagawea come along, even with her infant son (only two months old) in a cradleboard strapped to her back. It was one of the best decisions they ever made.

Sacagawea had been born about 1787 in present-day Montana or Idaho, a member of the Snake tribe of the Shoshone Indians. Around 1800, she was kidnapped by Minnetaree warriors who gambled her away to Charbonneau, who married her and another woman he also won. The family was in a Mandan village on the Missouri River when the Lewis and Clark Expedition arrived late in 1804 to spend the winter before continuing their four-thousand-mile journey to the Pacific Coast.

When the expedition set out again in April 1805, Lewis and Clark quickly learned that Sacagawea had excellent instincts as a guide and noticed that the Native Americans they encountered seemed to be reassured by seeing a woman leading. When they reached Shoshone country, where they feared hostility, Sacagawea discovered that her brother, whom she hadn't seen in years, had become chief of the tribe. After a tearful reunion with her family, she obtained the horses the expedition needed and a guide to lead them through the Rocky Mountains.

Sacagawea stayed with the expedition to the Pacific Ocean, and, on its return in 1806, she and Charbonneau left the company in present-day North Dakota. Almost nothing is known of the rest of her life. According to some records, she died somewhere near the Missouri River in 1812. But in 1875, an elderly woman claiming to be Sacagawea was discovered among the Wind River Shoshone in Wyoming. This woman died in 1884, which would have made Sacagawea almost one hundred years old.

Sacagawea's Importance

Many feel that without Sacagawea, the expedition would have been forced to turn back. There are many monuments to Sacagawea along the Lewis and Clark route. A mountain, a river, and a mountain pass were also named after her.

Let Me Introduce You . . .

In introducing the expedition leaders to tribal chiefs, Sacagawea called Lewis "Long Knife" and Clark "Red Hair."

Sign Language

There were nearly one hundred different languages spoken by the Native American tribes of the West, but they often managed to communicate with sign language. Here are a couple of examples:

1 To ask a question, you first have to sign that a question is coming. You do this by waving your open hand, fingers up, back and forth three or four times. "What's your name?" in Native American sign language is, first, the sign for a question, followed by "How you called?" as shown in the drawings.

Jean-Baptiste

According to some accounts, Sacagawea and Charbonneau took their son, Jean-Baptiste, to St. Louis and turned him over to Clark to be educated. Clark placed the boy in a school run by missionaries. Apparently Jean-Baptiste Charbonneau became a missionary, working among the tribes of the upper West.

QUESTION　　　HOW YOU　　　CALLED (KNOWN)

2 Sickness or a pain is signed by holding all 5 fingers of the right hand in front of the body and moving them in and out, as if they were throbbing.

3 Love: cross the wrists in front of the heart.

4 Astonishment or surprise: hold the palm of the left hand over the mouth.

5 Great hunger: hold the little finger of the right hand against the center of the body and move it from side to side.

6 Eat: with the right hand almost closed, pass the tips of the fingers in a curve downward past the mouth two or three times.

To learn more about Native American sign language, check your local library. In very little time, you will be able to sign and understand messages with a friend.

Wampum

Things You'll Need

newspaper or paper towels

1 cup water or rubbing alcohol

small bowl or measuring cup

red and blue food coloring

30 to 40 pieces of uncooked macaroni (or other shapes that have a hole through them)

spoon

yarn, 20 to 24 inches

One way Native Americans of different tribes traded with others was by using wampum as money. Wampum was often made of beads cut from the inner purple and white portions of clamshells. Since the purple was harder to cut and less plentiful, it had greater value than white wampum. The beads were strung on a piece of rawhide and often worn as a neck-lace. Make your own string of purple and white wampum.

1 Spread a newspaper or paper towels on your work surface. Pour about 1 cup of water or rubbing alcohol into a bowl or measuring cup. (It's okay to use water, but don't soak it very long or the macaroni will soften.)

2 Mix a little red and blue food coloring in the bowl to create purple.

3 Soak some of the macaroni in the purple dye, removing them with a spoon and placing them on the paper towel or newspaper to drain.

4 Make the purple a little darker by adding more food coloring, and color a few more pieces of macaroni. You can leave some uncolored to be white wampum.

5 When the beads are dry, string them on the length of yarn, mixing up the shades. Tie a square knot to complete the wampum necklace.

In Their Own WORDS

Can you imagine how my heart beat when he said that I could join the expedition? Here, after all the years, was a chance to see my own people again! At the thought of it I was so happy that I cried.

SEQUOYAH

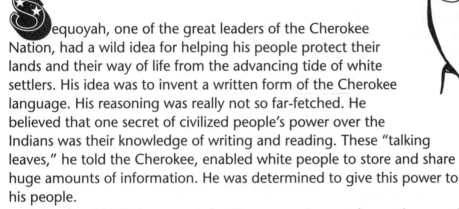

Born ca. 1770, London City, Tennessee
Died August 1843, Tamanlipas, Mexico

Sequoyah, one of the great leaders of the Cherokee Nation, had a wild idea for helping his people protect their lands and their way of life from the advancing tide of white settlers. His idea was to invent a written form of the Cherokee language. His reasoning was really not so far-fetched. He believed that one secret of civilized people's power over the Indians was their knowledge of writing and reading. These "talking leaves," he told the Cherokee, enabled white people to store and share huge amounts of information. He was determined to give this power to his people.

Born about 1770 in present-day Tennessee, Sequoyah was the son of a Cherokee woman and an English trader named Nathaniel Gist (or Guess). He became a skilled hunter and warrior, as well as a silversmith and a fur trader. He was injured while serving with the U.S. Army during the Creek War (1813–1814) and was lame in one leg for the rest of his life.

Beginning about 1809, Sequoyah worked for more than ten years to develop a Cherokee alphabet. He created eighty-six characters, each representing a separate syllable or sound. He used some characters from the English alphabet as well as some from Hebrew and Arabic scripts.

At first the Cherokee people thought he was ridiculous, but then he demonstrated how easily even young children could learn to read

and write, and the Cherokee were rapidly converted. By the late 1820s, thousands of Cherokee were communicating with written words, and they began publishing their own newspaper, the *Cherokee Phoenix*.

Although many white Americans supported the Cherokee cause, even the written language was not enough to protect the Cherokee from land-hungry settlers. In 1835, the Georgia government banned publication of the *Cherokee Phoenix*. The whites were determined to force the Cherokee to give up their lands and move beyond the Mississippi River. By the early

1840s, nearly all Cherokee had given up the struggle and joined the tragic march to "Indian Territory" (modern Oklahoma), a march the Cherokee called the "Trail of Tears." In 1843, Sequoyah traveled to Mexico to search for a Cherokee band that had apparently gone there during the American Revolution. He became ill and died there.

Building Words

In developing a written language, Sequoyah would create a symbol to stand for a sound. He then often found that many other words began with the same sound or syllable, so writers could use one symbol for the same sound in all words. In a similar way, your challenge in this activity is to see if you can find twelve words that begin with the sound **bar**. Use the clues and write the rest of the letters on the spaces.

1 A building for storing hay   B A R __

2 Long, low boat   B A R __ __

3 The part of a dog that's worse than the bite   B A R __

4 Hair cutter   B A R __ __ __

5 Cheap purchase   B A R __ __ __ __

6 Outdoor cooking   B A R __ __ __ __ __

7 A fence with sharp pieces   B A R __ __ __ __ __ __ __

8 To trade without money   B A R __ __ __

9 An uncivilized, crude person   B A R __ __ __ __ __

10 Device for measuring atmospheric pressure   B A R __ __ __ __ __ __

11 Singer with a low voice   B A R __ __ __ __

12 Person who mixes drinks   B A R __ __ __ __ __ __

Answers appear at the back of the book.

"We the Cherokee People . . . "

With Sequoyah's guidance, the Cherokee became the only Native American nation with a written constitution. Modeled after the United States Constitution, the preamble states:

We, the Cherokee People, constituting one of the sovereign and independent nations of the earth, and having complete jurisdiction over its territory . . .

However, very few white people paid any attention.

All the Way to the Supreme Court

When the state of Georgia nullified the Indians' title to their lands, the Cherokee, instead of fighting, took their case to the Supreme Court. In 1832, the Court's decision, written by Chief Justice John Marshall, declared that the Cherokee were the rightful owners. President Andrew Jackson, determined to force the Indians to move, responded: "Marshall has made his decision, now let him enforce it." Because the Supreme Court had no power to defend the Cherokee, the president defied its ruling and continued with the relocation.

Measuring the Trail of Tears

The map below shows the routes that many Native American tribes were forced to take to get to "Indian Territory," the land set aside by the U.S. government for Native Americans to settle. Use the map to answer the following questions.

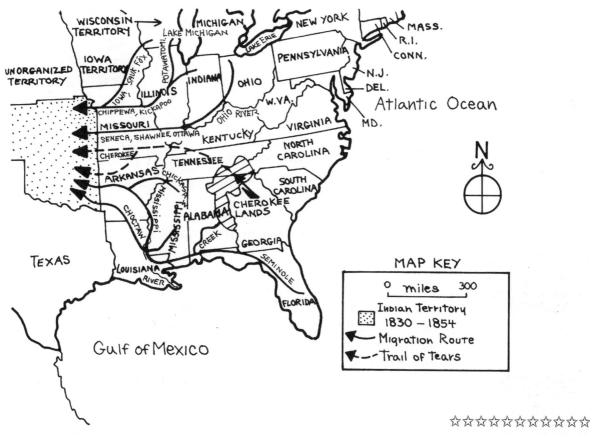

1 About how many miles did the Cherokee travel to reach the eastern edge of Indian Territory?

2 The hatch marks show the area of the Cherokee homeland. In what states did they live?

3 Name the other tribes that were forced to move to Indian Territory.

4 Which four tribes had the longest distance to travel?

Answers appear at the back of the book.

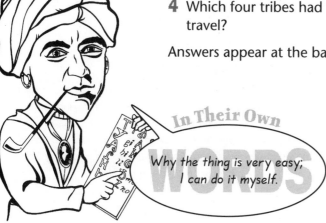

In Their Own WORDS

Why the thing is very easy; I can do it myself.

☆☆☆☆☆☆☆☆☆☆☆

The Big Trees

In the late 1800s, the giant redwoods of California's Sierra Nevada were named after the great Cherokee leader. Sequoyah National Park was created in 1890 to protect major groves of these trees, which are among the oldest and largest of the world's living things. The largest—the "General Sherman Tree"—is between three thousand and four thousand years old.

☆☆☆☆☆☆☆☆☆☆☆

ABRAHAM LINCOLN

Born *February 12, 1809, Hodgenville, Kentucky*
Died *April 15, 1865, Washington, D.C.*

Abraham Lincoln was a firm believer in America as the land of opportunity. But in his own case, he had enormous obstacles to overcome to make it work. He grew up in frontier poverty, moving from Kentucky to Indiana, then to Illinois. He was just nine years old when his mother died. He had few chances to go to school, but he made up for it by reading every book he could find, often walking several miles to borrow one.

As a young man in New Salem, Illinois, Lincoln worked a variety of jobs—rail-splitter, storekeeper, surveyor, and village postmaster. He volunteered for militia duty during the Black Hawk War in 1832, although he said his only enemies were the giant mosquitoes.

Lincoln studied law, then moved to Springfield, the state capital, to launch a political career. He served in the state legislature from 1834 to 1841, and then served a single term in the House of Representatives from 1846 to 1848. Lincoln failed to win reelection because he opposed the Mexican-American War. He married Mary Todd in 1842; of their four sons, only Robert lived to adulthood.

Lincoln withdrew from politics until 1854, when the Kansas-Nebraska Act propelled him back into politics with a new determination—to stop the spread of slavery into the new territories of the West. Although Lincoln did not feel the government had the authority to interfere with slavery where it already existed, his firm stand against its expansion led him to join the

Mary Todd Lincoln's War

First Lady Mary Todd Lincoln was suspected by some members of Congress of being a spy for the Confederacy. Their reason: she had four brothers and four brothers-in-law, all serving in the armies of the Confederacy.

☆ ☆

The First Assassination Plot

Critics made fun of Lincoln for sneaking through Baltimore at night on the way to his inauguration in 1861. But Lincoln had good reason for secrecy. A government agent named Harry Davies had infiltrated a band of eight would-be assassins who planned to kill the president-elect on his way through Baltimore. Davies revealed the plot to master detective Allan Pinkerton, who devised a way of avoiding the assassins by disguising Lincoln and slipping him onto a late-night train.

☆ ☆

new Republican Party in 1856. Two years later he challenged Senator Stephen Douglas in his bid for reelection. During his debates with Douglas, Lincoln warned that "'A house divided against itself cannot stand.' I believe this government cannot endure permanently half-slave and half-free." Douglas kept his Senate seat, but the seven debates between the two men made Lincoln a national figure.

Lincoln was elected president in 1860 and reelected in 1864. People were captivated by Lincoln's eloquence and his ability to explain complex issues in ways they could understand. These gifts served him well during the great national crisis of the Civil War (1861–1865).

From 1861 to mid-1863, the Confederate States of America seemed close to winning their independence. But Lincoln refused a compromise peace, insisting that the union of states be restored. His Emancipation Proclamation in 1863 gave Northerners the feeling that they were fighting to end the blight of slavery as well as to restore the Union.

After stunning Union victories at the battles of Vicksburg and Gettysburg in July 1863, the tide of the war changed. In his brief, eloquent Gettysburg Address in November of that year, Lincoln helped Americans understand why the war was necessary and noble. His unique leadership was a key to the nation's survival as a union of states.

In April 1865, just as the war ended, Lincoln was assassinated by John Wilkes Booth.

Lincoln's Duel

In 1842 a state official named James Shields accused Lincoln of slandering him in an unsigned newspaper article. When Lincoln denied involvement, Shields challenged him to a duel. The choice of weapons was Lincoln's, and he chose long swords. Apparently one look at the 6'4" Lincoln swinging a 6-foot sword was enough to cause Shields to back down.

Scrambled Civil War Terms

President Lincoln loved word games and brain teasers. He probably would have enjoyed unscrambling these words and then finding and unscrambling the eighth word, formed by the letters in the squares.

1 E P C A E   _ _ _ □ _

2 T T B A L E   _ _ □ _ _ _

3 O C N P R L A T M O I A   _ _ □ _ _ _ _ _ _ _ _

4 U N N O I   _ _ □ _ _

5 A Y L S E V R   _ _ _ □ _ _ _

6 D R M E F E O   _ □ _ _ _ _ _

7 O E C N R F D Y E C A   _ _ _ _ _ _ _ _ _ _ □

8 □□□□□□□

Answers appear at the back of the book.

Silhouette Portrait

© 2006 by John Wiley & Sons, Inc.

Throughout most of the nineteenth century, silhouettes were a favorite way to keep family portraits, especially for people who could not afford painted ones. A silhouette is a profile cut from dark material and mounted on a light background. The Lincolns would have had theirs done. (By the 1860s, the new technology of photography made photo portraits popular.)

1 Place the chair close to the wall and have your partner sit in it.

2 Place the light so it shines on your partner's profile. Darken the room and adjust the light so that a sharp profile appears on the wall.

3 Tape a piece of paper on the wall so that the profile is on the paper, as shown in the drawing. Make whatever adjustments are necessary to have the portrait in the size and position you want.

4 With your partner holding perfectly still, use a pencil to trace the outline of his or her shadow on the white paper. Cut out the profile and tape it to the sheet of black construction paper.

5 Trace around the profile with pencil and cut out the black silhouette.

6 Center the black silhouette on the second sheet of white paper, then glue it in place.

In Their Own WORDS

The world will little note nor long remember what we say here [at Gettysburg], but it can never forget what they did here.

30

FREDERICK DOUGLASS

Born *February 7, 1817?, Tuckahoe, Maryland*
Died *February 20, 1895, Anacostia Heights, Washington, D.C.*

In the 1840s, when Frederick Douglass first began giving speeches for an antislavery society, audiences were awed by his eloquent speaking style and his intelligence. But some people did not believe that this man could have emerged from a life in slavery. "It defies reason," one editor said. To quiet the critics, Douglass wrote his autobiography in 1845, when he was twenty-eight years old. *The Narrative of the Life of Frederick Douglass, an American Slave* was a best seller, and it is still considered one of the best sources of information about slave life.

Born in 1817 or 1818, Douglass was originally named Frederick Augustus Washington Bailey. While he was serving as a house slave in Baltimore, his owner's wife defied the law by teaching Frederick to read and write. When he was sixteen, his master died and Frederick became a field hand and, for a time, worked on ships.

In 1838, he managed to escape to the North, changed his name to Douglass, and became a speaker for the Massachusetts Anti-Slavery Society. After a speaking tour in England, he started his own newspaper, the *North Star* (later called *Frederick Douglass's Paper*) in Rochester, New York. During the Civil War, he was a consultant to President Lincoln, urging him to make slavery a central issue of the war and to arm freed slaves. After Lincoln issued the Emancipation Proclamation, Douglass actively recruited African American troops, including his two sons.

A brilliant speaker, an outstanding writer, and a tireless promoter of basic civil rights—including equality for women—Douglass was one of the towering figures of the nineteenth century. He served in several appointed government posts in the 1870s and 1880s. In 1889, he was named United States minister to Haiti, the first African American to represent the United States in another country. He died in 1895 in Washington, D.C.

Who Goes There?

At the gala celebration of Lincoln's second Inaugural, police officers stopped Douglass from entering the room. He managed to say to another guest, "Please tell the President that Fred Douglass is at the door." Moments later he was admitted with deep apologies. The officers had been unable to imagine that a black man had been invited to the White House.

A Prophecy

After the Civil War, Douglass continued to urge leaders not to disband the antislavery societies. He insisted that their work was not done, even after the passage of the thirteenth, fourteenth, and fifteenth amendments, which were designed to ensure the rights of African Americans. Douglass predicted that the Southern states, "by unfriendly legislation, could make our liberty . . . a delusion [and] a mockery." That's exactly what happened. By 1900 Southern states had passed laws that kept blacks segregated and unable to vote until the civil rights movement of the 1960s and 1970s.

Write Your Own Biography

Frederick Douglass was a young man when he first wrote his life story. You can start a little younger and make your own book. You can use it to write an auto-biography, or as a diary or journal to record a trip or a summer vacation, or to write a story.

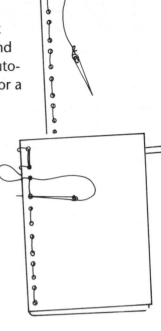

Things You'll Need

20 to 25 sheets of white paper, 8½ × 11 inches

2 sheets of sturdy construction paper in your favorite color for the cover

ruler and pencil

scissors or paper cutter (optional)

clamps or clothespins

cutting board or thick magazine

awl or hand drill (for adult's use only)

carpet thread or string

large sewing needle

adult helper

1 Sheet by sheet, fold the paper in half twice, so that the double sheets measure 4¼ inches × 5½ inches. You can leave the paper folded, or, if you prefer, cut it or carefully tear it along the folds to make single sheets. Repeat with the cover sheets.

2 Sandwich the sheets between the covers.

3 About ½ inch from the edge (or what will be the spine), make a vertical line of pencil marks about ½ inch apart. Use the clamps or clothes-pins to keep the sheets together, and place them on a thick magazine or cutting board.

4 Ask your adult helper to use an awl or a hand drill to make a hole through the cover, all of the sheets, and the back cover at the first pen-cil mark. Twist the awl back and forth to make a clean hole. Continue making holes at all of the pencil marks.

5 Cut a long piece of thread or string—about 36 inches—thread the nee-dle, and sew the book together: start at the bottom hole in the back and go up through one hole and down through the next. Continue to the top. Make the last stitch go around the top, then bring it up through the last hole, and go back in the opposite direction, as shown. Notice that at each hole, you go around the spine.

6 At the top, run the thread around the top, then tie the two ends firmly. Cut off any extra thread, and hide the knot inside the book.

Design a Newspaper Masthead

Newspapers often have very distinctive mastheads—the part that goes all the way across the top of the front page. This includes the name of the paper, often the subtitle, and some sort of catchy phrase or quotation. Other information such as the name of the city and, especially in the 1800s, some sort of symbolic drawing to represent liberty, justice, or another theme is included.

Try designing a newspaper masthead. This could be a publication for your city or town, for your school, or for some cause that you want to promote.

In Their Own WORDS

I'll fight slavery with my pen as well as my voice.

Harriet ★ Tubman

Born ca. 1820, Dorchester County, Maryland
Died March 10, 1913, Auburn, New York

Born into slavery in Maryland about 1820, Harriet Tubman endured a cruel master while working as a field hand. In 1849, she managed to escape to the North with the help of the Underground Railroad—an informal network of whites and free blacks who established safe houses and provided guides.

She herself then became the most famous "conductor" on the Underground Railroad, making nineteen trips into the South and helping more than three hundred slaves reach the North or Canada. She became known as the "Moses of her people" because she led them out of slavery.

Harriet Tubman had great physical strength and endurance, but her survival also depended on her courage, intelligence, and careful planning. She often said that she depended on two things: her faith in God and the loaded revolver she kept at her side. The fugitives who traveled with her quickly learned to rely on her. They knew she would not hesitate to use the pistol, and they believed her when she warned that "Dead Negroes tell no secrets!" No one ever betrayed her, and she never lost an escaping slave. Slave owners offered rewards of $40,000 for her capture. In 1857 she even managed to rescue her own family, including her elderly parents.

During the Civil War (1861–1865), Tubman worked for Union Army forces on islands off the coast of South Carolina, where the first African American regiment was being trained. She worked as a cook, laundress, and nurse, and was also a Union spy, going behind Confederate lines to gather information. On some missions, she also acted as a scout.

After the war, Harriet Tubman helped start schools for free slaves in North Carolina. She then returned to Auburn, New York, where she had established a home for poor former slaves. She remained in Auburn until her death on March 10, 1913.

Soldier Tubman

In 1864, a former minister named James Montgomery led a small band of African American volunteers from the Union Army in a raid deep into Confederate territory. Harriet Tubman helped plan the raid and served as scout. They returned with 727 slaves.

Change of Plans

In Canada in 1858, Tubman met John Brown, the fiery abolitionist who was planning to lead a raid on whites at Harpers Ferry, Virginia, hoping to spark a widespread slave uprising. Tubman was impressed by Brown and apparently planned to join him for the raid. Fortunately for her, she was ill at the time. The raid, in 1859, was a complete failure, and all the raiders were killed or captured. Brown was tried, convicted, and executed.

Word Honeycomb

Harriet Tubman was skilled at fitting clues together, a talent that helped her lead slaves to freedom and later to serve as a spy and a scout. Your challenge in this puzzle is to see how many words you can make with four letters or more.

Start with any letter and travel in any direction, collecting letters for a word as you go. The letters must be connected, but they do not have to be in order. For example, you can use the word **VERY** because all four letters are connected, but you could not use **PLENTY** because the letter **T** is not connected to the others. See how many you can find. A score of 20 is excellent; 15 is good. Answers appear at the back of the book.

Carryall Sack

Train travel was still new in the 1850s, and people devised a variety of ways to carry their belongings. Harriet Tubman used one of the most popular luggage forms—a carpetbag, made by sewing together old carpet scraps. Inside the carpetbag she carried several smaller bags for personal belongings, and in one of these she carried her loaded revolver.

Here's a project for making a simplified version of a popular carryall sack.

Things You'll Need

several sheets of newspaper

6-by-19-inch piece of felt, brown or dark blue (denim can be substituted)

pencil

ruler

scissors

hole punch

fabric glue or craft glue

stapler

twine or jute, about 24 inches long

small button

sewing needle

brown or blue thread

permanent black marking pen

1 Spread newspaper on your work surface and put the fabric on top.

2 Use the pencil and ruler to draw a rectangle on the fabric that is 6 inches wide and 19 inches long.

3 To make a flap for the sack, mark a pencil dot 2 inches in from each side of the fabric at the top edge. Mark two more dots 3 inches down each side edge. Connect the dots on each side with a pencil line (shown as the shaded area in the drawing); this will be folded later.

4 Cut out the pattern with the scissors. Also cut a small slit in the flap for a buttonhole.

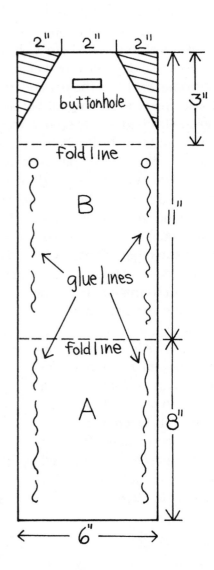

34

5 With the hole punch, make two holes in the fabric about 1 inch in from the sides and from the top fold line.

6 Spread glue along the sides of A and B, as shown. Fold A 8 inches onto B and press firmly in place for about 5 minutes. Reinforce the seam by putting five or six staples down each side.

7 Tie a double knot in one end of the twine. Thread the other end through both holes in B, keeping the knot inside the sack. Run the twine through the second hole and tie another double knot.

8 Fold the flap down and make a pencil mark through the slit to indicate where the button should be placed. Use needle and thread to sew the button firmly in place.

9 Use a marking pen to write your initials or name on the front of the sack.

Note: To make the sack strong enough for everyday use, ask an adult to help you sew the seams on a sewing machine.

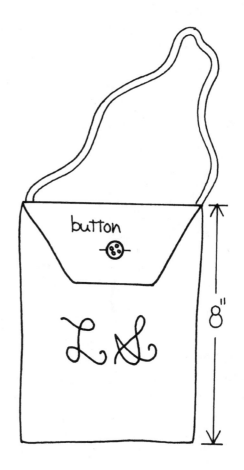

In Their Own WORDS

There are two things I have a right to, liberty or death. If I can't have one, I will have the other.

★★★

Born *February 15, 1820, Adams, Massachusetts*
Died *March 13, 1906, Rochester, New York*

In her day, Susan B. Anthony was one of the most unpopular women in America. She was a vigorous campaigner for women's rights at a time when most Americans, including women, were opposed to granting more rights to women. But to small numbers of women and to a few men then, and to many people now, Anthony was a great hero.

She was born in 1820 into a New England Quaker family, a family that made sure that being a woman would not prevent Susan from having an excellent education. She grew up as an independent, strong-willed individual with a strict moral outlook.

After teaching school in New York State for fourteen years, she returned to her parents' home in 1850 and became a speaker for an antislavery society. In 1852, she turned her energies to the *temperance* movement, which advocated moderation in the use of alcohol. Rebuffed by the all-male temperance society, she formed a temperance organization for women.

Anthony became best known for her unrelenting drive for greater equality for women, especially the right to vote. She was a gifted speaker and displayed great courage in facing taunts and insults from hostile audiences. In 1872, she famously defied the law by voting in the presidential election. She was arrested and fined $100. Anthony refused to pay the fine. "In your ordered verdict of guilty," she said to the judge, "you have trampled under foot every vital principle of our government!" The judge decided against a jail sentence because that would give her still more publicity. As it was, her symbolic act did gain nationwide attention, and she made the most of it in her speeches. "The Constitution of the United States," she told audiences, "refers to 'We, the People,' not to we, the male citizens." She never did pay the fine.

The "Anthony Amendment"

The Nineteenth Amendment has been called the "Anthony Amendment"—a fitting tribute to Anthony's crusade. And she actually did have a hand in the wording of the amendment many years before it became law. In 1878, she worked with a male supporter, Senator A. A. Sargeant of California, to find the simplest wording for such an amendment. The senator introduced the amendment in Congress, and the wording was never changed when it entered the Constitution forty-two years later.

The Great Petition Campaign

In New York, as in most states in the mid-1800s, women could not own property, and if they worked, their husbands controlled their wages. In a one-woman campaign to change this, Anthony traveled across the state by stagecoach, horse-drawn wagon, and train, carrying petitions to fifty-six of the state's sixty counties. In 1869, state legislators, awed by the support she had gained, passed laws granting women control over their property and wages.

© 20056by John Wiley & Sons, Inc.

In 1851, she joined forces with Elizabeth Cady Stanton, who had organized the first convention on women's rights in 1848. Together they led the women's rights movement for the next fifty years. She served as vice president and then president of the National Woman's Suffrage Association until 1900. Susan B. Anthony never married, devoting her energies to her crusade until shortly before her death in 1906. Her death came fourteen years before the Nineteenth Amendment finally gave women the right to vote in 1920.

Design a Coin

In 1979, the U.S. Mint issued the Susan B. Anthony coin, worth one dollar. The new coin was not a success. Paper dollars were preferred, and the coin's size made it hard to distinguish from a quarter. Most of the coins disappeared into people's collections.

Sketch a design for a new Susan B. Anthony silver dollar, front and back. Include a picture and words or a motto. Redraw your design on a piece of cardboard and cut it out, making your model a size you think would be easier for people to identify and use.

Scrambled Dates

Three years before Anthony voted illegally, Wyoming became the first state to grant women the right to vote in state elections, but not national ones. The United States did not ratify the Nineteenth Amendment until 1920. By that time, New Zealand's women had been voting for twenty-seven years. France did not extend voting rights to women until seventy-two years after Susan B. Anthony's protest vote, while England actually beat the United States by two years. Switzerland remained an all-male domain until French women had already been voting for twenty-seven years.

Work out the year in which women won the right to vote in each of the following:

England   Switzerland
France   United States
New Zealand   Wyoming

Answers appear at the end of the book.

In Their Own WORDS

May it please your honor, I will never pay a dollar of your unjust penalty. . . . "Resistance to tyranny is obedience to God."

37

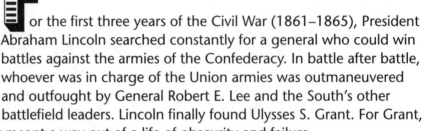

Ulysses S. Grant

Born *April 27, 1822, Point Pleasant, Ohio*
Died *July 23, 1885, Mount McGregor, New York*

For the first three years of the Civil War (1861–1865), President Abraham Lincoln searched constantly for a general who could win battles against the armies of the Confederacy. In battle after battle, whoever was in charge of the Union armies was outmaneuvered and outfought by General Robert E. Lee and the South's other battlefield leaders. Lincoln finally found Ulysses S. Grant. For Grant, the war meant a way out of a life of obscurity and failure.

Grant grew up on the family farm in Ohio until age seventeen, when he went to the United States Military Academy at West Point. He ranked near the bottom of the class of 1843 in everything except horsemanship. Assigned to the infantry, he performed heroically in the Mexican-American War (1846–1848). But after marrying Julia Dent in 1848, he languished in isolated frontier posts. Frustrated by the boredom and the long separations from his family, Grant resigned his commission in 1854.

After failing in several business ventures and at farming, Grant went to work as a clerk in his father's leather goods store in Galena, Illinois. The Civil War broke out in April 1861, but Grant had trouble getting the attention of the army. Finally given a small command early in 1862, Grant led assaults on forts Henry and Donelson in Tennessee. Working in tandem with navy gunboats, he scored two impressive victories—the first Union victories after nearly a year of war.

The following year, Grant displayed remarkable skill and daring in capturing the fortified city of Vicksburg, the last Confederate stronghold on the Mississippi River. After another brilliant victory at the battle of Chattanooga in November 1863, President Lincoln placed Grant in command of all Union armies. For the next year, Grant used the North's superiority in population and industrial might to pound the Confederate forces into submission. Casualties were shockingly high, but Grant finally forced Lee to surrender the main Confederate army at Appomattox Court House in April 1865.

Hailed as a great national hero, Grant was elected to two terms as president. He was an honest man himself, but he had a knack of surrounding himself with dishonest men. These men took advantage of him to steal money from the public treasury and were caught in a variety of scandals that shocked the nation. After Grant left the presidency, other "friends" took advantage of him in business dealings, leaving him deeply in debt. To restore his family's finances, Grant wrote his autobiography, a two-volume history of the war, which is still regarded as an outstanding work.

☆☆☆☆☆☆☆☆☆☆☆

Don't HUG Me

Originally, Grant's name was Hiram Ulysses Grant. He changed it for two reasons: First, the Ohio congressman who arranged his appointment to West Point couldn't remember his full name, so he used Grant's mother's maiden name, Simpson, as a middle name. Grant then dropped Simpson, but kept the S to become Ulysses S. Grant. As a boy, he had always hated the nickname kids gave him using his initials: HUG.

☆☆☆☆☆☆☆☆☆☆☆

He finished it as he lay dying of throat cancer. The book's publication provided his family with a substantial legacy.

Figure It Out

1 The siege of Vicksburg by Grant's army lasted from May 18 to July 4, 1863. Union artillery fired an average of 2,500 shells a day into the city. How many shells did they use? _____

2 The battle of Shiloh cost Grant's Union forces roughly 13,000 casualties (killed, wounded, and missing) out of about 30,000 at the start of the battle. The Confederates lost 11,000 out of 40,000. What percentage was lost by each side? _____

3 In the final siege of Petersburg (1864–1865), the Union lost 50,000 men, about 40 percent of their army; the Rebels lost 31,000, or 46 percent. Approximately what was the size of each army when the siege began? _____

Answers appear at the end of the book.

Caught Speeding

During his presidency, Grant was fined for speeding on the streets of Washington, D.C. He was driving a one-horse carriage!

Working with Map Colors

Maps were vital to those who planned the campaigns and battles of the Civil War. Colors were valuable for extra clarity; even while making sketches during a campaign, cartographers often used colors.

The mapmakers knew that on any map, it was important not to use the same color for adjoining items, such as states. They knew, too, that they could achieve this on any map using no more than four colors. That's your challenge on this map: color the states using only four colors, making sure that the same color is not used for adjoining states.

Hint: Make a rough selection by using numbers *before* you begin applying color.

In Their Own WORDS

The strategy of war is really quite simple: Find out where your enemy is. Get there as soon as you can. Strike at him as hard as you can and as often as you can, and keep moving on.

SITTING BULL

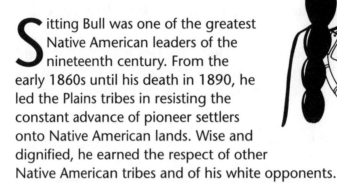

Born *ca. 1831, Sioux territory, South Dakota*
Died *December 15, 1890, Standing Rock Reservation, Wyoming*

S itting Bull was one of the greatest Native American leaders of the nineteenth century. From the early 1860s until his death in 1890, he led the Plains tribes in resisting the constant advance of pioneer settlers onto Native American lands. Wise and dignified, he earned the respect of other Native American tribes and of his white opponents.

Tatanka Iyotake was born in present-day South Dakota about 1831. He was a member of the Hunkpapa Sioux, a branch of the Dakota (or Teton) Sioux—the largest and most powerful of the Plains nations. As chief of the northern hunting Sioux, he accepted a U.S. government peace offer in 1868, but the treaty became worthless in 1874 when gold was discovered in the Dakota Black Hills. As thousands of whites joined the gold rush into Sioux sacred grounds, many Sioux, Arapaho, and Cheyenne flocked to Sitting Bull's Montana camp, looking to him for leadership.

By 1876, Sitting Bull was head of a war council for an estimated 4,000 warriors—the largest Native American force in history. Defying government orders to return to their reservations, Sitting Bull sent his two chief lieutenants—Crazy Horse and Gall—to meet the advancing U.S. Army. On

Sitting Bull and Custer

In an ironic twist, the rush of gold seekers that triggered Native American resistance and led to Custer's death at the battle of the Little Bighorn began after gold was discovered by an expedition led by Colonel Custer.

☆☆☆☆☆☆☆☆☆☆☆☆☆☆☆☆☆☆☆☆☆

Sitting Bull and Buffalo Bill

No matter what happened in the Indian Wars, the way of life of the Plains Indians was doomed by the destruction of the bison herds. Beginning in the late 1860s, professional hunters were hired by railroad companies to kill the buffalo to feed railroad workers. Others killed them for their hides and for sport. The most famous of the hunters was Buffalo Bill Cody, who once killed 4,280 bison in one eight-month stretch. It is one of the ironies of history that Sitting Bull's dear friend had helped to destroy the Sioux way of life.

☆☆☆☆☆☆☆☆☆☆☆☆☆☆☆☆☆☆☆☆☆

June 25, 1876, the Native American force met a cavalry unit led by Colonel George A. Custer at the battle of the Little Bighorn. Surrounded and hopelessly outnumbered, Custer and his entire command of more than 260 troopers were wiped out. It was the greatest Native American victory in the long history of the "Indian Wars," and very nearly the last.

Sitting Bull was well aware that larger army forces were coming, so in May 1877 he led his people into Canada, hoping to find a safe haven there. "So long as there remains a gopher to eat, I will not go back," he vowed. But the bison herds were no longer large enough to feed the Native Americans there, and the Canadian government was unable to help. After a four-year struggle, Sitting Bull led 187 of his people, sick and starving, back into the United States to surrender. After two years in prison, he was moved to Standing Rock Reservation. He left there for a year to tour with Buffalo Bill's Wild West Show. That event made Sitting Bull a legendary figure throughout the world.

After returning to the reservation, he encouraged a religious movement known as the "Ghost Dance." The movement convinced many of the remaining warriors that they could still drive the white people out of their lands. Under government orders, reservation police were sent to arrest Sitting Bull on December 15, 1890. When Sioux warriors tried to rescue him, he was accidentally shot and killed.

The Trained Horse

Buffalo Bill gave Sitting Bull the horse he had ridden in the Wild West shows, and the Sioux leader took the horse back to the reservation. When reservation police came to arrest Sitting Bull, the horse heard the shooting and thought it was his cue to go into his act riding in circles around Sitting Bull. The Sioux warriors, convinced that the spirit of their fallen leader had entered the horse, continued fighting.

Model Shield

Plains Indians made shields out of buffalo hide stretched over a wooden frame. The design painted on the shield displayed something important to the warrior's personal history. Eagle feathers were added because the eagle was more powerful than all other birds.

1 Staple the plates together.

2 On a piece of scrap paper, sketch the picture or symbols you want on your shield. It might be a bird or animal that you admire for its strength or wisdom or courage.

3 Copy the drawing onto the bottom of the double plate. Paint the design in your choice of colors.

4 Cut a strip of felt about 2 inches longer than the width of the shield. Staple the strip to either side of the shield on the back (the blank top of the plate).

5 Punch four or five holes around the bottom of the shield. Wrap a scrap of yarn around the shaft of a feather several times, and tie it, leaving one long piece to tie to one of the holes, as shown in the drawing. Repeat with the rest of the feathers.

Things You'll Need

2 large paper plates ("heavy duty")
stapler
scrap paper
pencil
acrylic or tempera paints
small brush
strip of brown felt, about 2 inches wide and 16 feet long
hole punch
scraps of yarn, any color
4 or 5 feathers (available at craft stores)

★ Word Surround

In the circle below, see if you can find all of the words, or parts of words, that are underlined in the following sentences:

The <u>Indian</u> <u>war</u>riors, most with <u>guns</u>, <u>surround</u>ed <u>Custer</u>'s <u>cavalry</u> column in the <u>year</u> 1876. The <u>Sioux</u> killed every <u>pony</u> <u>soldier</u> in the one-sided battle.

Answers appear at the back of the book.

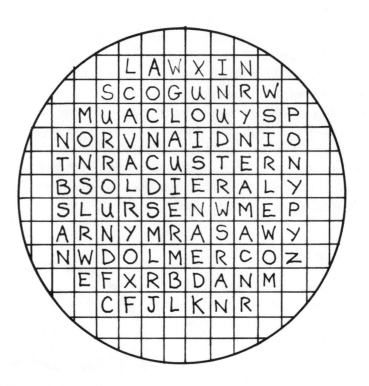

THOMAS ALVA EDISON

Born *February 11, 1847, Milan, Ohio*
Died *October 18, 1931, West Orange, New Jersey*

When Thomas Alva Edison was born in 1847, there was little practical use for electricity, except for the telegraph, which was developed by Samuel F. B. Morse. Edison changed that. His invention of electric lighting and of power-generating plants produced a revolution, making America a nation of electric lights, motors, and appliances.

Largely home-schooled by his mother, Edison became the perfect model of the brilliant, eccentric inventor, often working alone night and day while working out some problem. His first inventions were for improvements in stock-ticker machines and in the telegraph, earning the first of his record 1,093 patents. Even in those early years, he revealed the eccentricities of his genius. Nearly deaf from a childhood accident or illness, he could shut out the world. The day of his wedding to Mary, his first wife, he stopped at his shop to check on something—it was dawn before he remembered Mary!

His great period of inventing was from 1876 to 1900. With his invention of the phonograph in 1876—the first recording of sound—people began calling him the "Wizard of Menlo Park." (Menlo Park was where Edison had just opened what he called his "invention factory.")

Edison's incandescent lightbulb (1879) was another invention that caused a sensation, followed by the extraordinary achievement of a complete system for generating and distributing electrical power. He and his assistants invented and manufactured generators, insulated wire, electric meters, switches, and sockets. Other inventions included an electric railway, the basic apparatus for motion pictures, an improved storage battery, and improvements in manufacturing cement and mining iron ore.

After 1900 Edison enjoyed life as America's resident genius. His desire to have a hand in managing many of the companies that resulted from his inventions was not successful, because his mind did not focus well on the details of business. Most of his companies were merged into the General Electric Company. He spent the last thirty years of his life with Mina, his second wife; they divided their time between New Jersey and a winter home in Florida. When he died in 1931, plans for paying tribute to the great inventor by turning off all electricity had to be scrapped because the nation could no longer get by without electricity, even for 60 seconds.

The Phonograph Craze

The early, clumsy phonographs caused a nationwide sensation. "Phonograph parlors" were opened throughout the country, where people eagerly stood in line for a chance to hear a few minutes of recited poetry or fairy tales.

Edison the Writer

Edison's writings, often with drawings, filled more than 3,000 notebooks.

Flashlight from Scraps

© 2006 by John Wiley & Sons, Inc.

adult helper
penknife (for adult use only)
1 piece of single-strand wire, about 6 inches long (doorbell wire works well)
pliers—narrow (needle-nose), if possible
transparent tape
1 D battery
flashlight bulb

Edison often played with scraps of materials around his workbench, fitting them together in different ways to see what he could make. You can imitate his method in this project to make a working flashlight out of a few materials.

1 Ask your adult helper to use the penknife to scrape about 1 inch of insulation off each end of the wire.

2 Use the pliers to bend one end of the wire into a tight circle or coil. Tape the coil to the battery so that part of the wire touches the tiny circle on the bottom (the battery's negative terminal).

3 Use the pliers to bend the other end of the wire into a circle that fits around the grooves in the bulb. The wire may stay in place without tape, but if you use tape, make sure it doesn't cover the base of the bulb.

4 Tape the middle part of the wire to the side of the battery, but keep enough wire untaped so that you can bend it down to have the base of the bulb press against the positive terminal of the battery, as shown in the drawing. Try it. Anytime you press the base of the bulb to the top (positive terminal) of the battery, you should have light.

Apple Butter

apples, cut up, about 4 cups
adult helper
paring knife (for adult use only)
large saucepan
tap water
mixing spoon
collander
13-by-9-inch baking pan
¾ cup honey or sugar
¾ teaspoon cinnamon
2 tablespoons softened margarine or butter
MAKES 2 CUPS

Edison was known for his poor eating habits. He would often forget meals for hours, then stuff himself with his favorites. He was especially fond of sweet foods, including an apple butter like the following.

1 Wash the apples and have an adult cut them into small pieces, discarding the cores.

2 Place the apples in a large saucepan and add about an inch of water. Cover and cook until the apples are soft.

3 Use a mixing spoon to press the cooked apple through the collander into the baking pan.

4 Add the honey or sugar, cinnamon, and margarine or butter. Stir well.

5 Bake at 300 degrees for up to 1 hour until the apple butter is thick enough to spread with a knife. Stir every 10 or 15 minutes. Store in a lidded jar. Spread the apple butter on toast or use it as a topping for yogurt or ice cream.

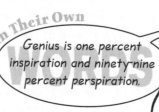

In Their Own WORDS

Genius is one percent inspiration and ninety-nine percent perspiration.

ALEXANDER GRAHAM ★★★★★★★★★★★★★ ★★★★★★

BELL

★★★ ★★★★

Born *March 3, 1847, Edinburgh, Scotland*
Died *August 2, 1922, Baddeck, Nova Scotia*

At the Philadelphia Centennial Exhibition in 1876, celebrating one hundred years of American independence, some visitors were struck by a small exhibit of a "speaking telegraph"—or telephone—by Alexander Graham Bell. When Dom Pedro, emperor of Brazil, tried it, he exclaimed, "Good Lord! It talks!" No one suspected how the country and the world would soon be changed by this invention.

Born in 1847 in Edinburgh, Scotland, Alexander Graham Bell emigrated with his parents to Canada in 1879, then moved to Boston. Bell's original career was working with the deaf, especially by teaching them speech, and he continued that work throughout his life. His mentor was Gardiner D. Hubbard, founder of the Clarke Institute for the Deaf, who encouraged his experiments in using low levels of electricity for the transmission of voice sounds.

After transmitting sounds that his assistant, Thomas A. Watson, could make some sense of, Bell applied for a patent on February 14, 1876—just hours before Elisha Gray sent a preliminary application for a very similar device. A few weeks later, while working with a liquid transmitter to improve his device, Bell spilled some acid and shouted, "Mr. Watson, come here! I want you!"—the famous first sentence transmitted by telephone.

The first demonstration of Bell's device at the Centennial Exhibition had been impressive, but at first no one knew how the telephone might be used. The president of Western Union, the largest telegraph company, called it "an electrical toy" that would never replace the telegraph. It took a couple of years to think of putting a telephone in every office and home. That's when Bell's invention became the most valuable patent in history.

Hubbard, whose daughter married Bell, helped him form the Bell Telephone Company in 1877. The company grew rapidly and spread to Europe. By the early 1880s, Bell had moved to Washington, D.C., where he pursued a variety of other interests. His great passion for the rest of his life was aviation. He also founded the journal *Science*, served as vice president and president of the National Geographic Society, and continued working with the deaf until his death in 1922.

The Assassin's Bullet

In 1881, when an assassin's bullet struck President James A. Garfield, doctors were unable to locate the bullet. When all else had failed, the family agreed to have Bell try to locate the bullet with a device he had invented for locating metal objects in the body. Bell's efforts failed, but the device remained useful until X-ray technology was developed.

Helen Keller

Bell met Helen Keller, a blind deaf-mute girl, when she was six years old. It was Bell who recommended that the family hire Anne Sullivan as her teacher. See the chapter on Helen Keller for more on how Anne Sullivan helped her to become one of the most extraordinary individuals of the twentieth century.

⭐ Telephone Secret Code

One of the most unusual uses of the telephone has been in sending and receiving secret messages. Several people, at different times in the early twentieth century, devised secret codes based on the telephone dial. Once the arrangement of numbers and letters on the dial became standard, designing a secret code was easy. Here's how it works:

Every letter is represented by two numbers, depending on its position on the dial, including its position in the cluster of three or four letters with each number. The letter A becomes 21—it's located at the number 2, and it's the first letter in the cluster. B = 22 and C = 23, and so on, through the alphabet. Zero can be used for Z (if it's not with 9).

Try deciphering the following message:

81-42-32   32-62-31   31-63-32-74   62-63-81   51-82-74-81-43-33-93

81-42-32   61-32-21-62-74

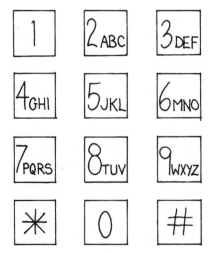

Answers appear at the back of the book.
Now try exchanging messages with a friend.

Backyard Telephone

Bell, Edison, and another inventor, Emile Berliner, wrestled with the problem of how to make use of the vibrations created by the human voice. In this project, you can use those vibrations to make two tin-can telephones.

1 Cut a round piece of strong paper about 1 inch larger around than the top of a can. (Use the can as a guide; the measurements don't have to be exact.)

2 Cut slits in the edge of the paper about 1 inch apart so that you can fold the paper tightly over the opening of the can. The slits should not extend over the opening of the can.

3 Repeat steps 1 and 2 to make another paper circle.

4 Use rubber bands to fix a paper circle firmly over one end of each can.

5 Use the needle to make a small hole in the center of each paper circle. Carefully push one end of the string through one hole and tie it to a toothpick. Do the same to the hole in the other can.

6 With a partner holding one can while you hold the other, stretch the string as tightly as possible. Take turns talking into one can while the listener holds the other can to his or her ear.

Things You'll Need

scissors
strong white paper
2 small clean tin cans with lids and bottoms removed
strong rubber bands
sewing needle
kite string—50 to 75 feet
2 toothpicks or small pieces of dowel

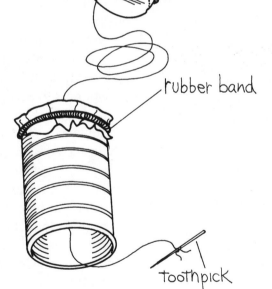

rubber band

toothpick

In Their Own WORDS

Leave the beaten track occasionally and dive into the woods. Every time you do so you will be certain to find something you've never seen before.

47

Booker T. Washington

Born *April 5, 1856, Franklin County, Virginia*
Died *November 14, 1915, Tuskegee, Alabama*

Throughout his life, Booker T. Washington believed that education was the key to a better life for African Americans. He was born a slave in rural Virginia in 1856. Emancipation led to freedom, but his family, like those of other freed slaves, was very poor. Washington began working at age nine, first in a salt plant, then a coal mine. He continued to work a variety of jobs in order to complete his schooling, graduating from Hampton Normal Agricultural Institute in 1875.

In 1881, after several years of teaching, Washington became the first principal of an agricultural school for blacks that he helped to start—the Tuskegee Institute in Alabama. Over the next thirty-four years, Washington built the school up from two buildings with no equipment and forty local students to an outstanding facility with one hundred well-equipped buildings, fifteen hundred students, and a faculty of two hundred. From the beginning, Washington told students to rely on themselves and not expect help from others.

Washington's outstanding work at Tuskegee made him the most famous African American at the turn of the century. The graduates of Tuskegee proved to be hard-working, with a strong sense of responsibility. Their willingness to accept racial segregation pleased white Americans. In a famous speech in 1895, Washington said that "in all things that are purely social, we can be as separate as the fingers, yet one as the hand in all things essential to mutual progress." More radical black reformers, such as W. E. B DuBois, rejected Washington's acceptance of segregation. They insisted that it was important to work for full civil rights and political participation.

In 1901, Washington founded the National Negro Business League. He also wrote several books, including two autobiographical works, *Up from Slavery* (1901) and *My Larger Education* (1911). He continued to insist that economic independence must come first, and that political and

A New Life

In his autobiography *Up from Slavery*, Washington described how different life was for him and other former slaves when they went to school after the Civil War:

> Life at Hampton was a constant revelation to me. The matter of having meals at regular hours, of eating on a tablecloth, using a napkin, the use of a bath-tub and a tooth-brush, as well as the use of sheets upon the bed were all new to me.

Dinner at the White House

In 1901, President Theodore Roosevelt invited Washington to dinner at the White House. It was a bold move on Roosevelt's part, and the invitation touched off a storm of protest from conservative white Americans. They remained convinced that blacks were inferior and should not be treated as equals. Washington was so self-assured that he was not bothered by the controversy. He became a consultant on race relations to Roosevelt and his successor, William Howard Taft.

civil rights would follow. Exhausted by years of overwork, Washington collapsed and died at Tuskegee on November 14, 1915, at the age of fifty-nine.

Pick-Up Sticks

In his emphasis on self-help, Washington taught young African Americans to make their own games and toys, using recycled materials when possible. You can do the same thing, making the game of pick-up sticks.

1 Spread the newspaper on your work surface and place the skewers on it.

2 Use the scissors to clip the sharp tips off the skewers.

3 Paint the skewers according to the following color scheme: 8 each of green, yellow, and blue; 14 red; 1 purple.

4 When the paint has dried, spray the pieces with clear enamel spray. (Do this outside or in a well-ventilated area.)

5 Cut a piece of gift-wrapping paper large enough to fit around the mailing tube. Spread a thin layer of craft glue around the tube. Carefully fit the paper onto the tube, pressing it in place. Use your decorated container to store the sticks.

Things You'll Need

2 or 3 sheets of newspaper
40 bamboo shish-kabob skewers
scissors
acrylic or poster paints in 5 colors: red, yellow, blue, green, purple
small brush
acrylic clear enamel (spray)
mailing tube, 18 to 24 inches long
gift-wrapping paper
craft glue or rubber cement
2 or 3 players

To Play Pick-Up Sticks

1 Bundle all the sticks together and stand them on end, holding the tops with your fingertips.

2 Raise them 2 or 3 inches above the table (or floor), then let go, letting the sticks fall in a random pile.

3 The first player tries to remove a stick from the pile without disturbing any of the other sticks. If the player moves any other stick, he or she loses the rest of the turn and the next player starts. Continue taking turns until all the sticks have been picked up. The player with the most sticks is the winner. You can also score by points: 1 point for each red; 2 points for each green, yellow, and blue; 10 points for purple; and 10 points for the last stick.

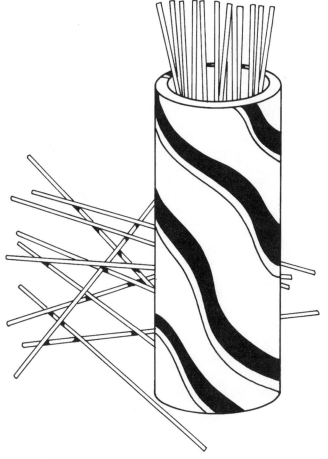

★ Build a Word

Figure out the words from each of the six clues and write your answers in the spaces. Each of the words has something to do with Booker T. Washington and his work. The letters in squares will form a seventh word that you have to unscramble to find a description of Washington.

1 The Civil War had finally ended the institution of _____.

_ _ ☐ _ _ _ _

2 The best thing Tuskegee could do for African Americans was to _____ them.

_ ☐ _ _ _ _ _

3 Washington felt African Americans should not ask for help but rather rely on _____.

_ _ _ _ _ _ ☐ _ _

4 Washington thought African Americans could wait for their civil _____.

☐ _ _ _ _ _

5 Segregation meant dividing people according to their _____.

_ _ _ ☐

6 For the time being, Washington said African Americans should accept _____.

_ _ _ _ ☐ _ _ _ _ _

7 _ _ _ _ _ _

Answers appear at the back of the book.

In Their Own
WORDS

No race can prosper till it learns that there is as much dignity in tilling a field as in writing a poem.

OLIVER WENDELL HOLMES JR.

Born *March 8, 1841, Boston, Massachusetts*
Died *March 6, 1935, Washington, D.C.*

Justice Oliver Wendell Holmes Jr. was one of the greatest individuals to serve on the U.S. Supreme Court. His famous written opinions were often dissents—statements opposed to the decision made by the Court's majority. But in time, many of his dissenting views came to be accepted as the law of the land—he was simply ahead of his time.

Holmes was born into one of New England's leading families. Surrounded by outstanding intellects like his father, Oliver Wendell Holmes Sr., Ralph Waldo Emerson, and Henry David Thoreau, he grew up with a desire to excel. The Civil War also had a powerful influence on him. When he graduated from Harvard in 1861, he became an officer in the 20th Massachusetts Volunteers. He was in several major battles and was seriously wounded three times. After a long courtship, he married Fanny Dixwell in 1872, beginning a happy marriage that lasted until her death fifty-seven years later.

After graduating from Harvard Law School in 1866, he spent most of the next decade practicing law and refining his legal philosophy. A series of his lectures, titled *The Common Law*, published in 1881, made him famous in Europe as well as the United States. A year later, he was appointed to the Massachusetts Supreme Judicial Court, where he remained until 1902 when President Theodore Roosevelt appointed him to the U.S. Supreme Court.

For the next thirty years, Holmes exercised a tremendous influence, both on the Court and on the thought of the nation. In one of his most famous opinions, written in a 1919 case, he argued that freedom of speech "would not protect a man in falsely shouting fire in a theater and causing panic." But, he continued, if the words did not present such a "clear and present danger," then they must be allowed. "The best test of truth," he wrote, "is the power of the thought to get itself accepted in the free marketplace of ideas," adding, "not free thought for those who agree with us, but freedom for the thought we hate." This view of freedom of speech has remained a basic tenet of American democracy ever since.

Holmes retired from the Court in 1932, when he was ninety-one years old. When he died in 1935, he willed his estate to the United States; it was used to finance a history of the Supreme Court.

Holmes's Lecture Fee

Holmes was often asked to give lectures and was pleased to accept a small payment. When he received an invitation to speak that contained no mention of a fee, Holmes responded: "I have at hand your kind invitation. However, I am far from being in good physical health. I am satisfied that if I were offered a $50 bill after my lecture, I would not have strength enough to refuse it."

★ Word Search

This word search puzzle contains ten words associated with the career of Oliver Wendell Holmes Jr. Can you find them all? Remember that the letters can go in any direction, including diagonal.

Answers appear at the back of the book.

COURT
SENTENCE
SUPREME
CASE
TRIAL
JUSTICE
JUDGE
LAW
MEDIATE
LEGAL

L	C	M	S	X	J	L	A	I	R	T
A	O	S	E	N	T	E	N	C	E	I
R	U	T	R	E	N	G	E	C	S	M
C	R	U	L	J	D	A	M	E	T	C
M	T	J	W	U	M	L	W	M	U	R
N	P	M	E	D	I	A	T	E	L	N
L	I	B	R	G	L	Y	S	R	G	A
D	T	R	M	E	D	A	I	P	L	W
J	U	S	T	I	C	E	T	U	N	J
Q	Y	L	M	N	D	R	B	S	I	C

Exercising Free Speech

During an early Civil War battle, Union soldier Holmes saw a tall, thin civilian standing in the line of fire. "Get down, you fool!" Holmes commanded. "You'll be killed!" The civilian turned out to be President Abraham Lincoln.

★ New England Clam Chowder

Although Holmes and Fanny had no children, he said that she "made my life poetry." That bliss included her cooking the traditional New England dishes they both enjoyed, like this very traditional New England clam chowder.

Things You'll Need

adult helper
2 medium-size potatoes
paring knife
cutting board
1 large pot
water
4 slices bacon
small frying pan
paper towels
onion chopper
1 onion
slotted spoon
one 10-ounce can whole baby clams
mixing spoon
measuring cup
1 cup half-and-half
1 cup whole milk
salt and pepper to taste
4 pats of butter (optional)
MAKES 4 SERVINGS

1 Ask the adult to help you wash the potatoes and cut them into small cubes. Place the potatoes in a large pot, cover them with water, and bring to a simmer.

2 While the potatoes cook, fry the bacon. When done, drain the bacon on paper towels, break the slices into small pieces, and add them to the potatoes.

3 Use an onion chopper or paring knife to dice the onion. Fry it in the bacon drippings and add to the potato-and-bacon pot with a slotted spoon.

4 Drain the clams into a measuring cup. Add the clams and half the juice to the pot.

5 Turn off the heat. Stir in the half-and-half a little at a time. Add the milk.

6 Turn up the heat almost to a boil and cook for about 5 minutes more. Add salt and pepper to taste. Many people like to place a pat of butter on the top of each helping.

In Their Own WORDS

Pretty much all the honest truth-telling there is in the world is done by children.

THEODORE ROOSEVELT

Born *October 27, 1858, New York, New York*
Died *January 6, 1919, Long Island, New York*

Theodore Roosevelt was considered a sickly child, but he went on to become a war hero, a president, and an amazing character. Everything about "Teddy" Roosevelt was larger than life. He lived what he called the "strenuous life"—boxing, hiking, rowing, swimming, hunting—and walked with such a furious stride that others had to jog to keep up. He spoke, one of his sons said, like a "human volcano" and always led the "laughter and singing and shouting."

But Roosevelt was also a serious scholar. He often read two or three books a day and found time to write twenty-four, including an outstanding three-volume history, *The Winning of the West*. He was considered an expert in several fields, including naval history and North American wildlife.

Born into a wealthy New York family in 1858, he was weak and sickly as a boy. But, through a rigorous program of exercise, he became a healthy, robust athlete. Soon after graduating from Harvard in 1880, he began climbing the political ladder by winning a seat in the New York Assembly. In 1884, his political career was put on hold when his wife and his mother died on the same day, January 14. For the next two years, Roosevelt lived the rough life of a cattle rancher in Dakota Territory.

Roosevelt returned to New York in 1886, remarried, and restarted his political career. He served as head of the U.S. Civil Service Commission (1889–1895),

☆☆☆☆☆☆☆☆☆☆☆☆☆☆☆☆☆☆☆☆☆☆☆☆☆

Things Named after Teddy

A wide variety of things were named after Roosevelt. The naming of the Roosevelt elk and the Roosevelt trout recognized his contributions to conservation. Most famous, of course, was the Teddy bear, inspired by a cartoon about his refusal to shoot a bear cub while hunting.

☆☆☆☆☆☆☆☆☆☆☆☆☆☆☆☆☆☆☆☆☆☆☆☆☆

president of the New York City Police Commission (1896–1897), and assistant secretary of the navy (1897–1898).

A strong supporter of the Spanish-American War (1898), he left his desk in the Navy Department to form his own cavalry regiment, the "Rough Riders." The unit was made up of his friends—Harvard graduates, athletes, and cowboys.

Roosevelt became one of the great heroes of the war when he led a charge up San Juan Hill in Cuba. This famous charge, featured in every newspaper in the country, was actually up Kettle Hill, smaller than San Juan and of less military significance. But it did add to Colonel Roosevelt's reputation, and weeks after the war's end he was elected governor of New York (1898–1900).

Elected vice president in 1900, Roosevelt became the country's youngest president when William McKinley was assassinated in September 1901. As the twenty-sixth president, Teddy Roosevelt provided an exciting, colorful, and progressive seven years in the White House. Roosevelt was the first president to attack the power and abuses of big business and to protect the consumer. Some of his most significant acts were in conservation. "The time has come," he warned "to inquire seriously what will happen when our forests are gone, when the coal, the iron, and the gas are exhausted, when the soils . . . [are] washed into the streams." Roosevelt transferred 125 million acres of land into forest reserve, while doubling the number of national parks, establishing fifty-one wildlife refuges and sixteen national monuments.

After leaving office in 1901, Roosevelt tried a comeback in 1912 but lost to Democrat Woodrow Wilson. He continued writing books and articles until his sudden death in 1919.

Roosevelt's Ranch Biscuits

Roosevelt operated his ranch when Dakota Territory was still wild and untamed. (He even managed to capture a gang of outlaws.) Baking soda biscuits were standard fare at the Roosevelt ranch house.

1 Put the flour in a large mixing bowl. Add the salt and baking soda. Mix.

2 Slowly stir in the cooking oil (saving a little to grease the cookie sheet) and sour milk until the mixture forms a soft dough. Add a little milk if it's too dry.

3 Roll out the dough on a bread board or countertop to a 1-inch thickness.

4 Dip the top of the glass in flour and use it to cut out 10 to 12 rounds (about 2 inches in diameter).

5 Place the biscuits on a greased cookie sheet, with the sides touching. Brush the tops with a little whole milk.

6 Bake at 400 degrees for about 15 minutes, until the tops are browned. Serve warm.

Handshake Record

As president, Roosevelt loved meeting the people and always insisted on shaking hands with as many as possible in any crowd. On New Year's Day, 1907, he established a record by shaking hands with 8,513 people.

 **Things You'll Need**

2 cups flour

large mixing bowl

1 teaspoon salt

1 teaspoon baking soda

wooden mixing spoon

2 tablespoons cooking oil, plus a little extra

¾ cup sour milk (add 1 tablespoon vinegar to milk, let it curdle for 10 minutes)

¼ cup whole milk

bread board or countertop

rolling pin

drinking glass for cutting out rounds

cookie sheet

pastry brush

MAKES 10 TO 12 BISCUITS

Backyard Bird Feeder

Teddy Roosevelt started bird watching when he was young, and while he was president he established the first fifty-one Federal Bird Reservations. Making a backyard bird feeder is a good way to begin learning about birds, and also to give your feathered neighbors some wintertime help.

Things You'll Need

hole punch (or awl and hammer)
1 or 2 disposable pie tins
adult helper
blunt scissors
twine
2 or 3 pine cones
5 or 6 tablespoons peanut butter
birdseed—mixed
guidebook of birds of North America
small notebook and pencil

1 Use a hole punch to make three equally spaced holes in the side of a disposable pie tin. If the hole punch is not strong enough to make the holes, ask an adult to help you with an awl (or other sharp instrument) and a hammer. To space the holes evenly, imagine that the pie tin is the face of a clock and space the holes 4 "hours" apart.

2 Cut three pieces of twine, each about 16 inches long. Thread one end of each through a hole in the pie tin and tie it in a firm square knot or double knot.

3 Pull the three ends of twine together above the pie tin and tie them together. Make sure the tin will hang level.

4 Tie a 12-inch piece of twine to the top knot to use for hanging the feeder to a tree limb.

5 Use shorter pieces of string to hang pine cones from the same three holes in your feeder. Spread peanut butter on each of the cones.

6 Fill your feeder with birdseed and ask the adult to help you hang it from a high tree limb.

7 Use the guidebook to help you identify the visitors to your feeder. Record each new bird and the date of the sighting.

In Their Own WORDS

Be practical as well as generous in your ideals. Keep your eyes on the stars, but remember to keep your feet on the ground.

Jane ★ Addams

Born *September 6, 1860, Cedarville, Illinois*
Died *May 21, 1935, Chicago, Illinois*

At the dawn of the twentieth century, thousands of immigrants faced hard times in America's fast-growing cities and industries. With little money or education, they found themselves living in overcrowded slum dwellings and working long hours at difficult jobs for low pay. Jane Addams wanted to help. She belonged to the first generation of college-educated women, many of whom became involved in social reform. In 1889, Addams and a college friend, Ellen Gates Starr, bought a large old house in a slum neighborhood of Chicago. They called it Hull House, and Addams, who never married, spent the rest of her life there.

Building on the English idea of a "settlement house," Addams set out to meet the needs of the poor neighborhood around Hull House by establishing a kindergarten, classrooms, a kitchen, a nursery, a playground, a workshop, and a gymnasium. All of these were free to anyone in the community, and young working women were able to live at Hull House. From the beginning, Addams attracted support from other social reformers, and the institution became a kind of laboratory for studying new social programs.

By 1910, more than one hundred settlement houses had been established throughout the country, all based on the Hull House model. Without knowing it at the time, Addams was helping to establish a new generation of professionals who would soon be known as social workers. The income Addams made from writing books and articles provided the funds she needed to keep Hull House going. Her most famous book, *Twenty Years at Hull House* (1910), became a classic work on social reform.

Addams recognized that improvement of her neighborhood, as well as the thousands of poor neighborhoods around the country, depended on better laws at the city, state, and federal levels. With the help of Hull House residents and supporters, she fought for laws to end child labor, make school attendance compulsory, recognize labor unions, and establish juvenile courts. She also worked for women's voting rights and was a founder of the NAACP (National Association for the Advancement of Colored People).

Addams became a vigorous peace advocate and opposed American involvement in World War I (1914–1918). After the war, she helped found the Women's International League for Peace and Freedom, serving as its president from 1919 until her death in 1935. In 1931 she was awarded the Nobel Peace Prize.

Using Every Opportunity

In her constant effort to improve conditions in the Hull House neighborhood, Addams even worked for a time as a sanitation inspector. She prowled the slums, making sure landlords had the garbage removed.

★ Word Clues

Unscramble each of the words below and write your answers in the spaces.
But notice that each word has one unused letter. Write these extra letters
in the column marked "Clues." The first one is done for you. When you've
unscrambled all the words, unscramble the clue letters to reveal the two-
word answer.

Clues

1 A large Midwestern city
 H I G C D A O C _ _ _ _ _ _ _   D

2 A rundown neighborhood
 M S L S U _ _ _ _

3 Bottom of a ship
 L H U L D _ _ _ _

4 Place where trials are held
 R C T A U O _ _ _ _ _

5 To improve
 M M O R E F R _ _ _ _ _ _

6 Under-age work
 D L I H C B R L O N A _ _ _ _ _ _ _ _ _ _

7 Person staying at Hull House
 D N A R T E S I E _ _ _ _ _ _ _ _

8 Chicago is a large one
 T E C I Y _ _ _ _

9 A family lives in a
 S J E U O H _ _ _ _ _

10 Not war but
 A C A P E E _ _ _ _ _

Answer: _ _ _ _ _ _ _ _ _ _

Answers appear at the back of the book.

More Than a House

From the single Victorian house they purchased in 1889, Addams
and Starr expanded their operations by buying neighboring
buildings and building new ones. By 1930, Hull House had
become a complex of thirteen buildings.

Butterfly Plant Decorations

The staff at Hull House taught crafts to neighborhood residents, giving them ideas for adding color and beauty to their homes. Here is a nifty way to add extra color to a potted plant, either in your own home or to give as a gift.

Things You'll Need

several sheets of newspaper

1 or 2 white mailing envelopes (like Tyvek), or substitute small round coffee filters

round drinking glass

pencil

ruler

scissors

3 or 4 small paper cups

tap water

food coloring—red, blue, yellow

toothpick, matchstick, or eyedropper

colored pipe cleaners

wood dowels

strong thread or fishing line

1 Spread the newspaper over your work surface and place the Tyvek-style envelopes on top. Use a large glass, or any round object, and pencil to mark four or five circles, each 4 or 5 inches in diameter. Small coffee filters will also work well. Cut out the circles.

2 Fill each paper cup with an inch or two of water. Add a few drops of food coloring to each cup. Colors should be bright. Mix colors to make green (blue and yellow) and purple (red and blue).

3 Using the food coloring, decorate the circles with colorful dots and lines to look like the markings on a butterfly. Use an eyedropper, toothpick, or matchstick to control single drops or short lines. Allow the circles to dry.

4 Pinch each circle in the middle and wrap one of the pipe cleaners around the middle. Twist the ends of the pipe cleaners into small tight circles to look like antennae, as shown in the drawing. Spread the sides of the circle to look like wings.

5 Stick the dowels into potted plants and attach the butterflies with thread or fishing line.

In Their Own WORDS

Action indeed is the sole medium of expression for ethics.

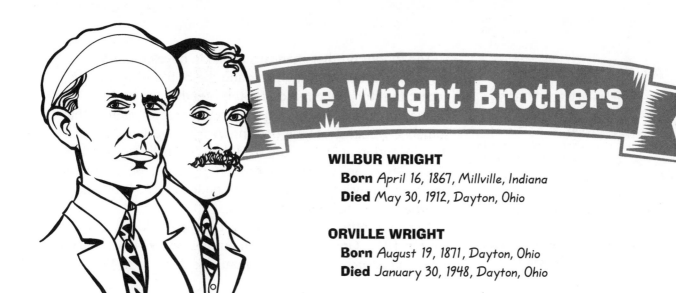

The Wright Brothers

WILBUR WRIGHT
Born *April 16, 1867, Millville, Indiana*
Died *May 30, 1912, Dayton, Ohio*

ORVILLE WRIGHT
Born *August 19, 1871, Dayton, Ohio*
Died *January 30, 1948, Dayton, Ohio*

Of all the people tinkering with the idea of human flight, Wilbur and Orville Wright might have been voted least likely to succeed. They were bicycle makers, not well-known scientists or inventors. And yet they managed to succeed where many others had failed.

The brothers grew up in a tightly knit family in Dayton, Ohio. Their father, a minister, was strict, but he also encouraged their explorations. After building a printing press and publishing a local newspaper for a while, Wilbur and Orville opened a bicycle shop in 1892. Soon they were manufacturing their own line of bicycles. Bicycles had been invented in the late 1870s, and in the 1890s a bicycle craze swept the country. This helped ensure the success of their business and provided the funds to finance their experiments in flight.

Beginning in 1899, the brothers built several aircraft—a kite, three gliders, and then three motor-powered airplanes. They went about their work with intelligence and extraordinary patience. In studying the failures of others, they realized that the problem of flight was really three related problems: (1) creating an engine powerful enough for liftoff but light in weight; (2) developing a plane surface over which air could flow, like the wing surface of a soaring bird; and (3) designing a system for steering the craft. When their first glider experiments failed, they concluded that the fault lay with the available information on aerodynamics (how a body or object moves through air). They experimented with different wing and tail designs and made nearly one thousand flights with their improved gliders, taking turns piloting the frail craft.

Their experimental work and tests at Kitty Hawk, a stretch of treeless sand on the North Carolina coast, gave them enough confidence to apply for a patent in March 1903. The patent was for a heavier-than-air motorized craft with their special "warped wing" design. After designing and building a 12-horsepower engine, they were ready to try the first manned, controlled, motor-powered flight by autumn 1903. On December 17, 1903, a wild, wintry day at Kitty Hawk, the brothers made history with four successful airplane flights. The longest was a flight of 59 seconds, covering a distance of 852 feet.

☆☆☆☆☆☆☆☆☆☆☆

Did Langley Succeed?

Samuel P. Langley of the Smithsonian Institution came closest to beating the two brothers. With the help of Alexander Graham Bell, he launched an unmanned craft from a houseboat on the Potomac River, using a catapult to get it into the air. It flew for three-quarters of a mile, but with no wing control, it plunged into the river. Then, just two weeks before the Wrights' success at Kitty Hawk, Langley's effort to launch a piloted plane failed when a wing tip caught the catapult and the plane crashed. Langley never tried it again.

☆☆☆☆☆☆☆☆☆☆☆

The Pace of Change

Airplanes became an instrument of war during World War I (1914–1918). Planes with machine guns and then with bombs were in action by early 1916. By 1920, the first airmail routes were established, and some mail planes would take a passenger or two who were willing to sit on the mailbags. True passenger planes began commercial flights in the late 1920s.

The Wright Brothers had succeeded in developing the first airplane, but both the press and the public were slow to accept the story. One reason for this was that the brothers spent the next two years improving their craft in secret, fearing that someone would steal their designs. When they demonstrated their invention in France, the world's press finally took notice. The brothers, an English writer reported, "are in possession of a power which will control the fate of nations." The brothers returned home to a hero's welcome.

Neither brother ever married. Wilbur died suddenly of typhoid fever in 1912. Orville retired from business in 1914 but remained active in research and consulting until his death in 1948.

Paper Airplane

 You'll Need

1 sheet of white paper
paper clip

Paper airplanes look easy to make. And they are, but it's also easy to make a mistake that produces poor results. Follow the instructions here to make a perfect paper airplane.

1 Fold the paper in half the long way, pressing the crease firmly. Place it flat on your work surface with the pointed edge of the crease facing up.

2 Fold the upper right-hand corner, marked *a*, down until it touches the center crease, as shown in the drawing. Press the new crease firmly. Do the same with the upper left-hand corner, marked *b*.

3 Fold point *c* over until it touches the center crease at *a*. Press the crease the whole length of the paper, as shown. Repeat with *d*, folding it to *b* and pressing the crease.

4 Pick up the airplane by the center crease. Raise the wings a little by lifting up points *c* and *d*.

5 Fit a small paper clip over the nose of the craft. Hold the airplane by the center crease to fly it. Use a firm, steady motion rather than trying to throw it hard. With a little practice, your airplane will soar surprising distances.

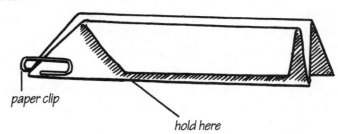

paper clip

hold here

Measuring Air Speed

From the beginning of their experiments, the Wright Brothers knew that the speed of the wind would have a powerful impact on flight. They tested their curved, or warped, wings by building the first wind tunnel, using a fan to push air through a tube, or tunnel. Later, when they tested their gliders and aircraft, one of the brothers would run alongside the craft holding an anemometer aloft to check the wind speed. Modern anemometers are similar to the model you'll make.

Things You'll Need

2 pieces stiff cardboard

scissors

4 small paper cups (the kind used in cup dispensers)

red felt-tip pen

white glue

large nail

spool for thread

block of scrap wood, such as a piece about 1-by-2 inches

long sewing needle

pencil with eraser

adult helper

1 Use scissors to cut two pieces of cardboard about 2 inches wide and 17 inches long. Cut a notch in the middle of each piece so they can fit together to make a cross, as shown in the drawing.

2 Use a red felt-tip pen to color one paper cup inside and out, then glue a paper cup to each of the four ends of the two crosspieces.

3 Make a hole in the center of the crosspieces with a nail. Remove the nail.

4 To make the base, fit the pointed end of a pencil into the hole in the spool. Glue the spool to the block of wood.

5 Attach the crosspiece to the base by putting the duller end of the sewing needle into the nail hole, then press the sharp end of the needle into the pencil eraser. Blow on the cups to make sure the anemometer turns easily. If it doesn't, make the nail hole in the crosspiece a little larger.

6 Place your anemometer outdoors on a level surface to see how the spinning cups change with increases or decreases in wind strength. You can measure this by counting how many times the red cup passes you each minute. Keep a record of the changes. An airport anemometer has an electronic counter that measures the spins in knots per hour or miles per hour.

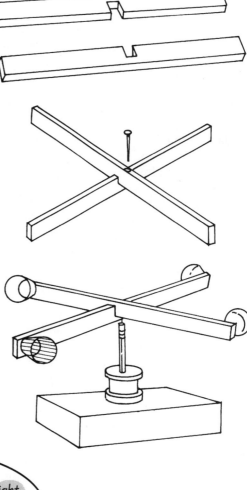

In Their Own WORDS

For some years I [Wilbur] have been afflicted with the belief that flight is possible to man. My disease has increased in severity and I feel that it will cost me an increased amount of money if not my life.

W. E. B.
DU BOIS

Born *February 23, 1868, Great Barrington, Massachusetts*
Died *August 27, 1963, Accra, Ghana*

"Beauty in Black"

As editor of the journal *Crisis*, Du Bois urged African American writers and artists to see "beauty in black"—that is, to promote African American culture and life. In the late 1960s, many African Americans developed an artistic and fashion movement called "Black Is Beautiful."

From the early 1900s until the civil rights movement in the 1960s, W. E. B. Du Bois was the leading voice for racial equality in the United States. He was also a brilliant writer, historian, and sociologist who helped Americans understand the nature of their country's racial conflict.

He was born William Edward Burghardt Du Bois in 1868 of African, Dutch, and French descent. His family encouraged his thirst for education and, after graduating from Fisk University in 1888, he earned a Ph.D. from Harvard in 1895. Over the next decade he completed several sociological studies of African American life.

Early in his career, Du Bois thought that the social sciences, like sociology, could help solve issues. At the dawn of the twentieth century, however, society was becoming increasingly segregated. New laws prevented African Americans from voting. These conditions led Du Bois to advocate protest.

In 1903 he published *The Souls of Black Folk*, attacking Booker T. Washington's idea of accepting racial segregation until African Americans achieved economic self-sufficiency. Speaking out against Washington was a bold move, and the book thrust him into the leadership of African American demands for change. "We want the Constitution of our country enforced," he insisted. "We want our children educated." In 1905, he led the founding of the Niagara Movement, a small organization that opposed Washington's stance. The movement broke up but paved the way for blacks and some whites to form the NAACP (National Association for the Advancement of Colored People) in 1909.

Du Bois became the NAACP's director of research and the editor of its magazine, *Crisis*, positions he held from 1910 to 1934. During the 1930s, Du Bois became increasingly radical by insisting on faster, more sweeping change. He began to advocate "Pan-Africanism"—the idea that all people of African descent should work together. He encouraged the development of African American art, literature, and music. His African American nationalism led him to resign from *Crisis* and the NAACP, and his belief in creating economic cooperatives led him toward communism.

He spent the 1940s teaching and doing research at Atlanta University. After another brief stint with the NAACP, he became more closely identified with the communist Soviet Union. During the 1950s, when anti-communism was very strong in the United States, Du Bois found himself shunned by many of the people who had considered him a great hero. In 1961 he moved to Ghana in Africa. He died there in 1963.

From Clues to Quotation

Figure out the answer to each clue and write it on the numbered spaces. Then transfer the letters to the corresponding numbers in the quotation. The answer will tell you the subject of Du Bois's lifelong crusade. Some letters in the quotation can be used in more than one clue. The first one has been done for you.

Clues

A) Not *in*, but _____

A) $\dfrac{O}{9} \quad \dfrac{U}{6} \quad \dfrac{T}{1}$

B) A bookcase has more than one _____

B) $\dfrac{}{4} \quad \dfrac{}{2} \quad \dfrac{}{3} \quad \dfrac{}{18} \quad \dfrac{}{16}$

C) A group of sheep make a _____

C) $\dfrac{}{10} \quad \dfrac{}{12} \quad \dfrac{}{5} \quad \dfrac{}{14} \quad \dfrac{}{15}$

D) A toy set of building _____

D) $\dfrac{}{11} \quad \dfrac{}{7} \quad \dfrac{}{17} \quad \dfrac{}{14} \quad \dfrac{}{19} \quad \dfrac{}{8}$

E) Front and _____

E) $\dfrac{}{11} \quad \dfrac{}{13} \quad \dfrac{}{14} \quad \dfrac{}{19}$

Quotation $\dfrac{T}{1} \ \dfrac{}{2} \ \dfrac{}{3} \quad \dfrac{}{4} \ \dfrac{}{5} \ \dfrac{U}{6} \ \dfrac{}{7} \ \dfrac{}{8} \quad \dfrac{O}{9} \ \dfrac{}{10} \quad \dfrac{}{11} \ \dfrac{}{12} \ \dfrac{}{13} \ \dfrac{}{14} \ \dfrac{}{15}$

$\dfrac{}{16} \ \dfrac{}{17} \ \dfrac{}{18} \ \dfrac{}{19}$

Answers appear at the back of the book.

Design a Historical Marker

Du Bois was born in Great Barrington, Massachusetts, a town that takes great pride in its history. But there is no monument or any other marker to indicate that he was born there. Design a roadside marker commemorating the birthplace of W. E. B. Du Bois and add a few lines about his life.

In Their Own WORDS

The problem of the twentieth century is the problem of the color line.

Albert Einstein

Born *March 14, 1879, Ulm, Germany*
Died *April 18, 1955, Princeton, New Jersey*

Albert Einstein was such a poor student in school that his parents worried there was something wrong with him. He made up for it by studying on his own, finding an outlet for his restless mind in mathematics and physics. He became the most influential scientist of the century and reluctantly played a key role in unleashing the awesome power of nuclear energy.

Even while he was finishing his schooling in Switzerland and working toward his Ph.D., Einstein proved to be an independent and original thinker. In 1905 he published a series of papers that astounded the world of science and mathematics. The papers included the famous mass-energy equation, $E = mc^2$. He was awarded his doctorate the same year and became a professor of mathematics and physics, teaching at several institutions before moving to the University of Berlin.

In 1916, Einstein published the results of his continuing investigations, pulling ideas together to produce what is regarded as his major achievement, his general theory of relativity—the theory that both time and motion are relative to the observer. He was awarded the Nobel Prize for physics, and from that time on he worked to produce an even grander synthesis called a "unified field theory."

When Adolf Hitler and his Nazi Party took control of Einstein's native Germany in 1932–1933, the Jewish scientist emigrated to the United States. He joined the Institute for Advanced Study at Princeton University, where he remained for the rest of his career. In 1939, concerned about rumors that Germany was developing an atomic bomb, Einstein wrote a letter to President Franklin Roosevelt warning that the Germans might be close to developing "extremely powerful bombs of a new type." He urged the president to provide government help to current university research. Roosevelt responded by creating the Manhattan Project, which led to the speedy development of the world's first atomic bombs.

After the first bombs were dropped on Hiroshima and Nagasaki, Japan, in 1945, Einstein was horrified by the scale of the destruction and the lingering danger of radioactive fallout. From that time until his death in 1955, Einstein devoted much of his energy to working for world peace.

Einstein for Peace

Einstein's work for world peace did not begin with his reaction to the first atomic bombs. In 1933 he had published a book titled *Why War?* His co-author was the famous psychoanalyst Sigmund Freud.

Einstein, the Plumber

Einstein was sometimes frustrated by the clumsiness of bureaucracy and the problems that created for his work. He once told a reporter that if he could start his life over, he would prefer to be a plumber, an electrician, or maybe a peddler—anything so that he wouldn't have to deal with officials.

Science Mystery Letter

In this puzzle, you have to find the mystery letter to add to each cluster of three letters, then unscramble the letters to find a four-letter word that can be associated with scientific experiments. Remember that the mystery letter must be the same for each group.

1 _ _ _ _   4 _ _ _ _

2 _ _ _ _   5 _ _ _ _

3 _ _ _ _   6 _ _ _ _

Answers appear at the end of the book.

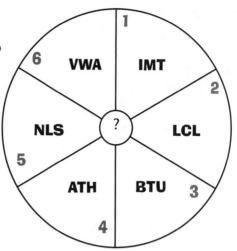

Finding the Center of Gravity

Einstein was intrigued by gravity and developed a theory about what causes it. While there is not an experiment to test his theory, you can try the following experiment to demonstrate a neat way to find the center of gravity of an object.

1 Cut the piece of cardboard into an uneven or irregular shape. Punch four holes in the edge of the cardboard at four random locations.

2 Use the push pin to attach the cardboard to the bulletin board by pushing the pin through one of the four holes. Tie one end of the string to the push pin and attach a washer to the other end. The string should extend down in front of the bulletin board, and the washer should swing freely.

3 When the washer stops moving, use the ruler and pencil to mark a line on the cardboard next to the string.

4 Move the push pin to one of the other holes and repeat the procedure in Step 3. Repeat this for the other two holes.

5 Remove the cardboard. The point where all four lines come together is the center of gravity. Place the cardboard on your index finger exactly where the lines cross. The cardboard will balance on your finger.

Things You'll Need

piece of light cardboard or
  manila folder
scissors
hole punch
push pin
bulletin board
string, about 12 inches long
metal washer
ruler and pencil

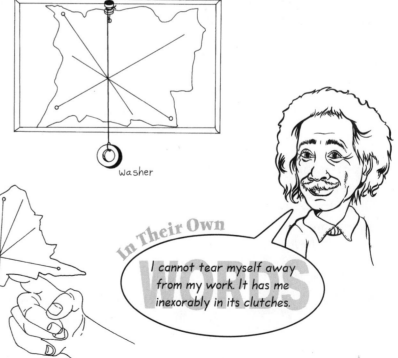

washer

In Their Own WORDS

I cannot tear myself away from my work. It has me inexorably in its clutches.

HELEN KELLER

Born *June 27, 1880, near Tuscumbia, Alabama*
Died *June 1, 1968, Westport, Connecticut*

© 2006 by John Wiley & Sons, Inc.

Breaking Taboos

In the early 1900s, blindness was a taboo topic for women's magazines. A courageous editor named Edward W. Bok accepted an article by Helen Keller for *Ladies' Home Journal*. The piece was immediately popular, and other major publications quickly followed by printing her articles.

Appreciating Music

Helen Keller could appreciate music. She "listened" by placing her hand on a piano, violin, or other instrument and feeling the vibration.

When Helen Keller was nineteen months old, illness suddenly plunged her into a world of darkness and silence. For the next five years Helen was like a wild, angry animal, striking out at everything and everyone around her. "I was a phantom living in a no-world," she later recalled. She remained blind, deaf, and mute for the rest of her life. However, with the help of a remarkable teacher, Helen became an extraordinary author and lecturer, and an inspiration to millions.

Alexander Graham Bell, one of the great experts on deafness, examined Helen when she was seven and encouraged the family to hire twenty-year-old Anne Mansfield Sullivan to teach her. That began a profound relationship that lasted through Miss Sullivan's marriage and ended only with her death fifty years later, in 1936.

Sullivan used remarkable patience, especially in those first weeks, when Helen fought everything. Finally, with water pouring on her hand, Helen felt Sullivan use her finger to spell the word "water" on the palm of Helen's hand. That was the first breakthrough—things had names, and Helen could learn them. That day, Helen Keller said in later years, "was my soul's birthday." With patience and courage on the part of both, Helen Keller learned to feel objects and associate them with words spelled out by finger spellings on her palm. She learned Braille, then sign language, and slowly learned to speak by feeling the position of the tongue and the lips, making sounds, and imitating the motion of lips and tongue.

In an age when most severely disabled people were placed in asylums, Helen Keller was able to attend Radcliffe College. She graduated with honors in 1904, having developed skills far beyond anything considered possible for a person with her disabilities. She began to write of her experiences; her autobiography, *The Story of My Life* (1902), is still in print in many languages more than a century later. She wrote several other books and numerous magazine articles.

In 1913 she began lecturing, mostly for the American Foundation for the Blind. Her intelligence, sensitivity, and courage provided an object lesson on how much disabled people were capable of. With Anne Sullivan's help, Helen Keller toured the country and the world, raising millions of dollars to aid the deaf and the blind, and inspired the formation of commissions for the blind in thirty states by 1937. Her work had a powerful influence on the treatment of the blind and the deaf. Above all, she is remembered for her courage and determination.

★ Say It with Feeling

Without sight or hearing, Helen Keller relied heavily on her sense of touch. Anne Sullivan spent the first two years having Helen feel objects and learn to identify them. In this activity you can work with a partner to try a similar experience.

1 Sit across a table from each other with one person blindfolded.

2 The sighted person picks up an object and gently brushes it across the cheek of the blindfolded partner, who then tries to guess what it is.

3 Place correct guesses in one pile. Take turns and see who is best at guessing the objects. Try other experiments with smell or taste.

★ **Things You'll Need**

a variety of soft objects:
  cotton balls
  piece of flannel
  piece of linen
  sponge
  glove
  feather
  handkerchief
  dish towel or clean rag
    for a blindfold

★ Visible Speech

One of the methods Helen Keller used to communicate was American Sign Language, called Ameslan, with the signs made in her hands so that she could feel them. Think of how hard it would be to speak in Ameslan without being able to see. The picture shows a few Ameslan symbols. With a friend, see how fast you can memorize all of them well enough to use. Then see if you can use them to communicate without looking by making the signs in each other's hands.

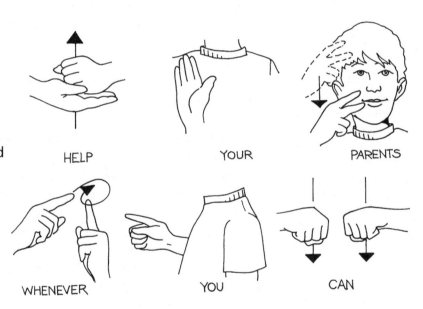

HELP   YOUR   PARENTS

WHENEVER   YOU   CAN

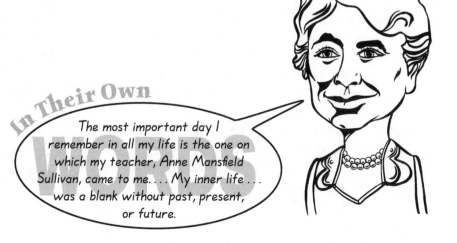

In Their Own WORDS

The most important day I remember in all my life is the one on which my teacher, Anne Mansfield Sullivan, came to me. . . . My inner life . . . was a blank without past, present, or future.

FRANKLIN D. ROOSEVELT

Born *January 30, 1882, Hyde Park, New York*
Died *April 12, 1945, Warm Springs, Georgia*

Franklin Delano Roosevelt, the thirty-second president of the United States, led the country through two great crises of the twentieth century: the Great Depression and World War II (1939–1945). With imagination, humor, political shrewdness, and a powerful personality, he gave Americans the confidence and the leadership the times required. He was both the most loved and the most hated of our presidents.

Roosevelt was born into an aristocratic New York family and attended private schools, then Harvard, and finally Columbia Law School. One of his mentors was Theodore Roosevelt, a distant cousin, whose niece Eleanor he married in 1905. He served as assistant secretary of the navy under President Woodrow Wilson and was the unsuccessful Democratic candidate for vice president in 1920. A year later, his political career appeared to be over when he was stricken with polio, which left his legs permanently paralyzed.

With tremendous courage and the inspired help of Eleanor, FDR gained enough mobility to resume his career. He won the governorship of New York in 1928 and 1930. In 1932, during the darkest days of the Depression, he was elected president, promising Americans a "New Deal." The nation was in the grip of fear and despair. Factories were closed, millions were unemployed, and once-prosperous families were facing hunger. No one knew what Roosevelt meant by his New Deal, but they believed him when he said his administration would "take a method and try it. If it fails, admit it frankly, and try another. But above all, try something!"

The country was close to panic when he took the oath of office in March 1933. In a flurry of activity that became known as the "Hundred Days," he turned the government into a great social

Roosevelt's Military Career

In 1898, Roosevelt and a fellow student decided to run away and join the army for the Spanish American War. They made their getaway in a bakery wagon loaded with pies. They both became ill, not from the pies, but from measles. That was the end of Roosevelt's military career.

Fala and Major

After Roosevelt's beloved dog Fala, a Scotty, died, the president acquired a German shepherd named Major. But Major managed to bite both British Prime Minister Ramsay MacDonald and Canadian Prime Minister Mackenzie King. Major no longer greeted visitors after that.

laboratory, trying one program after another. Some people objected to these programs.

Some New Deal programs provided immediate relief, putting people to work on government projects like building dams, highways, and parks. Other programs were designed to correct weaknesses in the economy, like insuring bank deposits and providing price supports for farmers. And some programs, like Social Security, were designed to give working people a degree of economic security. The New Deal legislation, combined with the reassuring radio voice in Roosevelt's "Fireside Chats," rapidly restored the nation's confidence.

Despite the success of Roosevelt's programs, the country did not fully emerge from the Depression until the huge military buildup required to fight World War II from 1941 to 1945.

Roosevelt proved to be a skilled wartime leader, overseeing a complicated worldwide strategy. He was elected to a third term as president in 1940 and a fourth in 1944. Exhausted by more than twelve years as president, Roosevelt died suddenly at his retreat in Warm Springs, Georgia, in 1945, four months before the war ended.

Word Search

This word search puzzle contains fourteen terms connected with FDR and the New Deal. See how many you can find.

WORK	DEPRESSION	JOBS
RELIEF	TVA	HUNDRED
DAYS	CHAT	BANKS
CABINET	LAW	RADIO
NEW	DEAL	

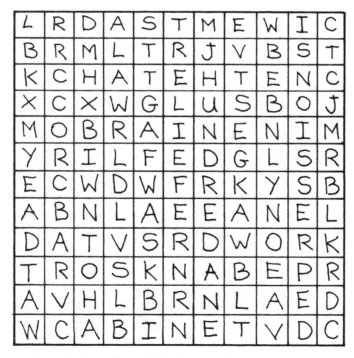

Answers appear at the back of the book.

Food for Fala

© 2006 by John Wiley & Sons, Inc.

Things You'll Need

1½ cups cornmeal

1¾ cups all-purpose flour

½ cup powdered milk

1 teaspoon baking soda

1 teaspoon salt

2 mixing bowls

sifter

large mixing spoon

measuring cup

egg beater or electric mixer

2 beef bouillon cubes

2 chicken bouillon cubes

water

3 eggs

adult helper

cookie sheet

waxed paper

cutting board

knife

pancake turner

airtight container (glass or plastic)

Roosevelt's little Scotty Fala was his nearly constant companion for years. We know that the dog was pampered by the president and the White House staff. Pamper your favorite dog with the crunchy treats you'll make in this activity.

1 Preheat the oven to 300 degrees F. Ask an adult to help.

2 Combine the cornmeal, flour, powdered milk, baking soda, and salt. Sift these dry ingredients into a mixing bowl.

3 Crumble the chicken and the beef bouillon cubes. Dissolve each flavor in ¼ cup hot water. Combine these two liquids with the eggs in the second mixing bowl. Stir to mix the eggs.

4 Slowly add the wet ingredients to the dry ones. With an adult's help, use the mixer to blend the ingredients until they become doughy.

5 Divide the dough into two flat, oval loaves, about 12 inches long. Place the loaves on a cookie sheet lined with waxed paper. Bake for about 50 minutes, or until the loaves feel firm to the touch. Remove from the oven and cool for 10 minutes.

6 Place the loaves on a cutting board and ask the adult to help you cut them into ½-inch slices. Return the slices to the cookie sheet and bake for 25 minutes. Flip the pieces over with a pancake turner and bake for another 25 minutes.

7 Turn off the oven and let the biscuits cool with the door propped open a little. The biscuits should be crunchy, providing your favorite dog with a gourmet treat. Store them in an airtight container.

In Their Own WORDS

The only thing we have to fear is fear itself.

Frances Perkins

Born *April 10, 1882, Boston, Massachusetts*
Died *May 14, 1965, New York, New York*

Two events in the early 1900s propelled Frances Perkins into a lifelong career of social reform. The first was working at Hull House with Jane Addams. Her experience there inspired her to go back to college, where she earned a master's degree in social economics in 1910. A year later, while she was studying the working conditions for women and children, she witnessed a tragic fire at New York's Triangle Shirtwaist Factory, in which 146 workers, mostly women, died, largely due to the negligence of the factory owners. From that time on, her life was devoted to the health and welfare of workers.

For twenty years, from 1912 to 1932, Perkins worked for the New York State Industrial Commission, the first woman to serve on the commission, and the first, in 1928, to become the state's industrial commissioner. Under her leadership, the state steadily improved working conditions and placed limits on the hours of work for women. She married Paul Caldwell Wilson in 1913 but kept her own name. Wilson suffered from a serious mental illness and spent many years in an institution, leaving the raising of their son in her hands.

When Franklin D. Roosevelt was elected president in 1932, he invited Perkins to become secretary of labor, the first woman to serve in a Cabinet—the group of advisers who are closest to the president. Perkins accepted, but only with the assurance that Roosevelt was committed to the two projects most important to her: help for those thrown out of work and more protection for workers on the job. Roosevelt agreed, and Perkins

Perkins and the First Lady

Perkins formed a close working relationship with First Lady Eleanor Roosevelt. They used public appearances together to encourage women to become involved in politics. They also helped convince the president to bring more women into his administration.

Perkins's Views on FDR

Perkins's book, *The Roosevelt I Knew*, published in 1946, became a long-running best seller. Perkins had known Roosevelt better than almost anyone, and readers were struck by her analysis of the man. Like many others, she found FDR to be "the most complicated human being I ever knew," but she also understood the qualities that made him so special. She saw, for example, that he had "a capacity for living and growing that remained until his dying day."

became the chief architect of two of the most important and lasting New Deal projects: the Social Security Act and the Fair Labor Standards Act.

Roosevelt relied heavily on Perkins, one of only two Cabinet officials who remained through his three-plus terms. She was popular with workers and labor unions, but others disliked her, especially some members of Congress and leaders of industry. She survived their attempts to push her out of the Cabinet and remained one of the most reliable figures in the New Deal.

After Roosevelt's death in April 1945, Perkins resigned her government position. After several years on the U.S. Civil Service Commission, she became a professor of industrial and labor relations at Cornell University. She died in New York City in 1965.

Alphabet Vegetable Soup

Things You'll Need

adult helper
2 onions, chopped
paring knife (to be used by an adult)
onion chopper
1 potato, chopped
1 cup celery, chopped
1 cup carrots, chopped
cutting board
2 tablespoons butter
2-quart soup pot
large mixing spoon
1 can beef stock
1 cup water
one 32-ounce can of tomatoes
1 box frozen peas
2 tablespoons parsley, chopped
½ teaspoon basil
¼ teaspoon thyme
salt and pepper
alphabet noodles
Makes 4 servings

The dozens of programs that Perkins helped establish were known by the letters of each program. For example, the Social Security Board was called the SSB. Other "alphabet agencies" were the TVA (Tennessee Valley Authority), the PWA (Public Works Administration), and the FDIC (Federal Deposit Insurance Corporation). People often referred to the programs as "Roosevelt's Alphabet Soup."

To honor Perkins and the alphabet agencies, here's an easy recipe to try.

1 Ask the adult to help you peel the onions (under cold running water) and cut them in quarters. Use an onion chopper to chop them into small pieces.

2 With the adult's help, dice the potato, celery, and carrots. Set them aside on the cutting board.

3 Melt the butter in the soup pot and sauté the onions.

4 When the onions are soft, add the beef stock, water, tomatoes, chopped vegetables, peas, and seasonings. Simmer for 1 hour.

5 Add the alphabet noodles and simmer for another 10 minutes. Serve hot.

Build a Word

Listed below are several words that are associated with the career of Frances Perkins. Figure out the word needed to complete each sentence and write the letters in the spaces provided. The letters in squares form another word, a scrambled one. When you unscramble it, you will have a word that describes Perkins's goal for Americans.

Cabinet	secretary	employment	Congress
fair	labor	unions	Practices

1 One of her goals was a law enforcing Fair Employment _____.   _ _ _ _☐_ _ _

2 FDR's closest advisors formed the _____.   _ _ _ _ _ _☐_

3 The key thing about employment laws, she thought, was that they be _____.   _ _☐_

4 Perkins was the secretary of _____.   _ _ _ _☐

5 One source of strength for workers was labor _____.   ☐_ _ _ _ _

6 The head of a cabinet department was the _____.   ☐_ _ _ _ _ _ _ _

7 Laws about employment were passed by the _____.   ☐_ _ _ _ _ _ _

8 One major economic goal was full _____.   _ _ _ _ _☐_ _ _ _

Answer: _ _ _ _ _ _ _ _

Answers appear at the back of the book.

In Their Own

WORDS

I came to Washington to work for God, FDR, and the millions of forgotten, plain common working men.

ELEANOR
ROOSEVELT

Born *October 11, 1884, New York, New York*
Died *November 7, 1962, New York, New York*

Eleanor Roosevelt's parents died during her childhood, and Eleanor grew up in the home of her grandmother, attending school in England. Even after her 1905 marriage to Franklin, her distant cousin, she felt isolated and insecure. "I was afraid to do anything," she later wrote, "even to drive a car." She overcame her fears to become the most active First Lady in history and one of the leading political figures of the twentieth century.

Eleanor's marriage to Franklin created a remarkable partnership. She managed to raise five children while also giving Franklin tremendous support in his struggle to overcome the crippling effects of polio. During this challenging period, she schooled herself in political matters and helped her husband win the governorship of New York and then, in 1932, the presidency.

As First Lady, "the Missus" (as FDR called her) became his "eyes, ears, and legs," traveling the country to assess the successes and shortcomings of the New Deal programs that her husband had put into effect. She became a skilled politician, learning how to use persuasion and personal connections to get things done. She also championed causes that were dear to her, especially the rights of women and minorities, and the needs of the poor throughout the world. Her daily column, "My Day," was printed in more than one hundred newspapers over a period of more than twenty years, and her books, magazine articles, and speeches were highly influential.

Code Names

During World War II, the Secret Service code name for FDR was "Cargo" because he had to be carried; Mrs. Roosevelt was "Rover" because of her constant travel. The president always had a revolver at his bedside, and the First Lady carried one in her purse. Agents gave code names to the guns, too: "His" and "Hers."

☆ ☆

A Lady of Principle

In 1939, the conservative Daughters of the American Revolution (DAR) refused to rent their Constitution Hall to the famous singer Marian Anderson because she was African American. Mrs. Roosevelt used her widely read "My Day" newspaper column to criticize that decision and to announce her resignation from the DAR. She then arranged for the concert to take place on the steps of the Lincoln Memorial.

☆ ☆

During World War II (1941–1945), Eleanor Roosevelt traveled to the war zones to visit the men and women in uniform. After her husband's death in April 1945, President Harry S. Truman named her a delegate to the newly formed United Nations. One of her proudest achievements was convincing the Soviet Union's delegate to support the U.N. Declaration of Human Rights in 1948. Even after resigning her United Nations position in 1953, Mrs. Roosevelt continued to travel widely, consulting with government leaders on the humanitarian issues that concerned her. When she died in 1962, she was widely regarded as the most admired and influential woman of the twentieth century.

⭐ E(asy) R(ecipe) Scrambled Eggs

By her own admission, Eleanor Roosevelt was a terrible cook. She once shocked the press corps by serving hot dogs to the king and queen of England, explaining that it was one of the two meals she could prepare. The other E. R. dish was scrambled eggs. She cooked the eggs in a chafing dish for whoever was at the presidential residence on Sunday morning. Here is the kind of recipe the First Lady could manage.

1 Break the eggs into a mixing bowl, add the milk, and stir well with a fork or whisk.

2 Add the salt, paprika, and pepper. Mix well.

3 Melt the butter in a large frying pan over medium heat. When the butter is hot and the edges start to turn brown, add the eggs and continue cooking over low heat. Some cooks prefer to continue stirring while the eggs cook; others insist the eggs should not be touched except to turn them once with the spatula, much like an omelet. When the eggs are firm but not dry, serve them on a small platter.

⭐ Things You'll Need

6 eggs
¼ cup milk
mixing bowl
fork or whisk
½ teaspoon salt
dash of paprika
¼ teaspoon pepper
large spoon
2 tablespoons butter
large frying pan
spatula
small serving platter
MAKES 3 TO 4 SERVINGS

⭐ Daily Journal

Eleanor Roosevelt filled dozens of notebooks with her observations, ideas, things she had overheard, and thoughts on important news events. Personalize your own notebook and use it to write about important events in your life.

1 Spread the newspaper on your work surface. Place the construction paper on it. Open the notebook and center it on the construction paper.

2 Trace a line around the notebook. Then use the ruler and pencil to draw another line about 2 inches from the edges of the notebook. Cut out the construction paper along the outer lines.

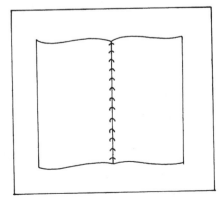

⭐ Things You'll Need

several sheets of newspaper
large piece of colored
  construction paper, about
  12 by 14 inches
small spiral notebook, about
  6½ by 9 inches
pencil
ruler
scissors
white glue
gold or silver pen

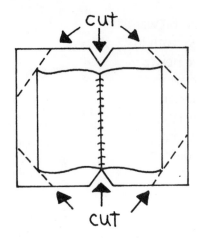

cut

cut

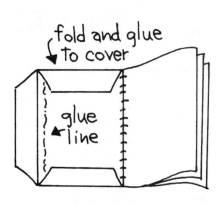

fold and glue to cover

glue line

3 Cut off the corners of the construction paper, as shown in the drawing. Clip a small triangle at the top and bottom in the middle of the paper in line with the spiral.

4 Fold the edges around the covers of the notebook. Close the notebook and run your thumb along the crease to shape the cover to the notebook. Open and close the notebook several times to make sure the fit is snug.

5 With the notebook open, spread glue on the edges of the inside cover that will be covered by the construction paper. Fold down each of the six flaps and press them into place.

6 Use gold or silver ink to write your name on the cover and a title for your journal, such as "My Journal," "My Day," or "My Trip."

My Journal

In Their Own WORDS

It isn't enough to talk about peace. One must believe in it. And it isn't enough to believe in it. One must work at it.

Babe Ruth

Born *February 6, 1895, Baltimore, Maryland*
Died *August 16, 1948, New York City, New York*

Born into a troubled Baltimore family, George Herman Ruth spent most of his childhood at St. Mary's Industrial School. A friendly priest helped the big, husky boy and encouraged him in his love of baseball. When he was nineteen, Ruth was signed by the Baltimore Orioles, who sold his contract to the Boston Red Sox later the same year. Ruth soon became the greatest player of all time.

Over the next four years, "the Babe" proved himself one of the best left-handed pitchers in baseball history. One of his proudest records was pitching $29\frac{2}{3}$ consecutive scoreless innings for Boston in two World Series (1916 and 1918). But it was as a hitter that he astounded the world, and it was as a larger-than-life personality that he became one of the dominant figures of the rollicking "Roaring Twenties."

In 1920, the owner of the Boston Red Sox sold Ruth's contract to the lowly New York Yankees. In later years, this sale became known as the cause of a curse on the Red Sox—a curse that, year after year, seemed to make it impossible for Boston to win the World Series and that became known as the "Curse of the Bambino."

From 1920 to 1934, Ruth led the New York Yankees to ten World Series, setting fifty-four records along the way, including the most home runs in a 154-game season (60 in 1927) and in a career (714), runs batted in (2,209), bases on balls (2,056), and strikeouts (1,330). As a player, his feats thrilled packed stadiums year after year, and the magnificent Yankee Stadium became known as "the house that Ruth built." Everybody loved this

By Any Other Name

Ruth was called "Babe" because of his youth (and baby face) when he signed with the Boston Red Sox in 1914 at age nineteen. He was also called "Bambino"—Italian for *baby*. Another nickname, the "Sultan of Swat," came from the way he "swatted" the baseball like a king or sultan (or because it sounded good with *swat*). There actually was a country of Swat, now part of Pakistan, and it was ruled by a sultan.

Incidentally, the Baby Ruth candy bar had nothing to do with the great slugger. It was named for the granddaughter of the president of the Williamson Candy Company.

77

overgrown manchild and his countless heroic feats, like hitting a home run for a hospitalized boy or pointing to the spot where he was about to hit a World Series home run.

Baseball historians consider Ruth the greatest player of all time for several reasons: (1) He was the only player in the game's history to master both the defensive (pitching) and the offensive (batting) sides of the game. (2) His home run hitting changed the very nature of the game, from an emphasis on defense and scoring one run at a time to a game of power. (3) He dominated the game as no other player before or since. And (4) he helped restore the public love for the game following the Black Sox scandal of 1919–1920, when several Chicago players were found guilty of "throwing" the World Series (losing on purpose for money).

Ruth loved his fame and the adulation of "the kids." He was never able to fulfill his dream of managing a team, but he did help many charities and established the Babe Ruth Foundation for Underprivileged Children. The "Curse of the Bambino" continued long after Ruth's death in 1948. The Red Sox lost several close World Series until finally in 2004, eighty-six years after their last championship, the Red Sox won the series in what fans called "the reverse of the Curse."

Comparing Greatness

Some modern baseball fans insist that today's players are better than those of the past. What do you think? Choose a player you think might rate higher than Ruth. It might be a player in the twenty-first century, like Sammy Sosa or Alex Rodriguez, or someone in the 1900s, perhaps Joe DiMaggio, Willie Mays, or Roberto Clemente.

Use the library or Internet resources to make your comparison. Some things to think about:

★ Consider raw statistics, such as number of home runs and also number of games.

★ Decide what other statistics you want to compare, such as batting average, runs batted in, strikeouts, and bases on balls.

★ Consider some of the factors that are not statistics. For example:

   ★ The number of years Ruth was a pitcher and his record as a pitcher.

   ★ Are today's players in better physical condition? Does that make a difference?

   ★ Today's players have luxury accommodations—but they also play many night games.

Babe Ruth's Baseball Hot Dog

Hot dogs were one of the Babe's favorite foods, and he could easily down a dozen. He liked them with everything on them, as in the following recipe:

1 Spray the skillet or add the cooking oil. Have an adult help you cook the ground beef loose over medium heat.

2 Chop the onion into small pieces and add to the skillet when the beef is nearly cooked. Continue cooking over low heat for 5 minutes.

3 Stir in the vinegar, sugar, ketchup, mustard, water, steak sauce, and salt. Cover and simmer for 15 minutes. If the sauce becomes watery, remove the cover and continue simmering until it's thicker.

4 Fill the saucepan halfway with water and have an adult help you bring it to a rapid boil. Puncture the hot dogs with a fork and use the tongs to lower them into the boiling water. Turn off the heat right away and let the hot dogs stay in the hot water for 5 minutes.

5 Use the tongs to place the hot dogs on rolls. Spoon some sauce on top of each hot dog. Serve warm with lots of napkins.

Things You'll Need

large skillet with lid

cooking spray or 2 tablespoons cooking oil

adult helper

1 pound extra-lean ground beef

onion chopper or cutting board

paring knife

1 medium-size onion

2 tablespoons each of vinegar, sugar, and ketchup

1 tablespoon each of dry mustard and water

1 teaspoon steak sauce

½ teaspoon salt

mixing spoon

medium saucepan

6 hot dogs

6 hot dog rolls

fork and kitchen tongs

MAKES 4–6 SERVINGS

In Their Own WORDS

The only real game in the world, I think, is baseball.

AMELIA EARHART

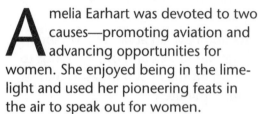

Born *July 24, 1897, Atchison, Kansas*
Died *July 2, 1937?, Central Pacific*

A melia Earhart was devoted to two causes—promoting aviation and advancing opportunities for women. She enjoyed being in the limelight and used her pioneering feats in the air to speak out for women.

Earhart's early life was marked by restlessness, perhaps a longing for excitement or challenge. She was born in Kansas, but the family moved often during her childhood. She completed high school in Chicago, served as a nurse for the Canadian army in World War I, and then was in and out of college, training to be a social worker. Ignoring her family's protests, she learned to fly in her early twenties.

In 1928, when she was thirty, she became the first woman to fly across the Atlantic Ocean, but as a passenger, not a pilot. As she described it, she was "just a sack of potatoes." But that was enough to give her the urge to be a pioneer aviator. She devoted herself to flying and quickly became known as a pilot and as an inspiring role model for women. She became aviation editor for *Cosmopolitan* and published two books on flying. In 1932, she made a solo crossing of the Atlantic, setting a record of just under fifteen hours. When she married publisher George Palmer Putnam in 1931, she kept her maiden name. She also continued flying, setting several altitude, speed, and distance records for women, and became vice president of Luddington Airlines, one of the early passenger services. With her short-cropped hair and athletic good looks, she seemed the ideal symbol of women's achievements.

In 1935, Purdue University hired Earhart as a career counselor for women. She was also the university's aviation consultant, and the institution provided her with a twin engine Lockheed Electra. The plane had such advanced technology that she called it her "flying laboratory."

Earhart set out on a round-the-world flight in 1937, with Frederick Noonan as her copilot. The first attempt ended with an accident in Honolulu, but the Electra was not badly damaged and they set out again. On

The Search for Amelia Earhart

The search for some evidence of what happened to Earhart and Noonan continues to this day. The most recent findings of airplane wreckage are tantalizing but, so far, inconclusive. She added to the mystery by leaving a letter for Putnam "just in case" she didn't return. "Please know," she wrote, "I am quite aware of the hazards. . . . Women must try to do things as men have tried."

© 2006 by John Wiley & Sons, Inc.

July 2, 1937, on one of the longest legs of the journey, they were trying to fly 2,556 miles from New Guinea to Howland Island in the central Pacific. The plane apparently had trouble. Radio contact was broken, and the plane disappeared. No trace of the aircraft or the fliers was ever found. The tragic ending added an element of mystery to the Amelia Earhart story. Rumors continued for years that she might still be alive somewhere.

★ Numbers Sequence

Amelia Earhart had to plan her journeys carefully, deciding how far they could travel between stops. She also had to measure the distance between fueling stations. In this puzzle, you will use that kind of sequence thinking to get from start to finish.

This is a two-step sequence. The first step is to add 2, and the second step is to add 4. We've done the first two steps for you. Follow the same sequence, adding 2 and then 4, from start to finish. You can't cross your path and you can't move through any square.

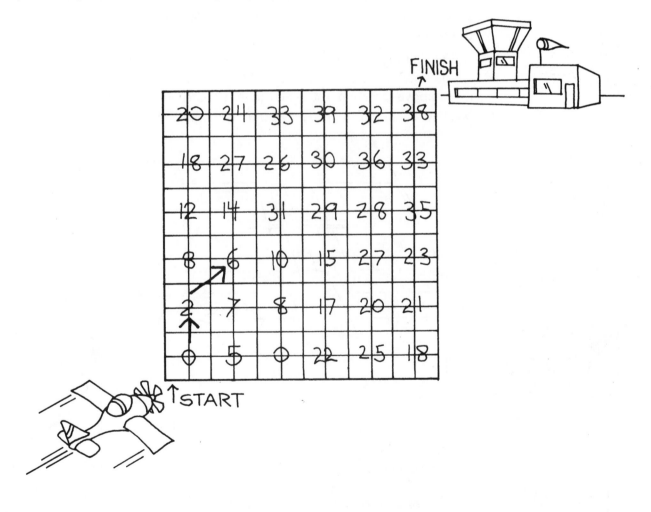

Answers appear at the back of the book.

Testing Lift on Aircraft Wings

Like other pioneer pilots of the 1920s and 1930s, Amelia Earhart studied the science and mechanics of flight. Pilots knew, for example, that it was important for the top of the wings to be curved. The reason: the air going over the top of the wing has to travel farther than the air passing underneath the wing, so the air has to move faster. That lowers the air pressure above the wing, giving the plane what is called *lift*. Here is a way to demonstrate lift.

1 With an adult's help, cut a paper towel tube in half with the sharp knife, then cut it lengthwise with the scissors, giving you two short curved pieces. Push down a little on one side of the curve to produce a shape like an airplane wing. The side that has more curve will be the front of the wing.

2 Place the two books near the edge of the table, about 3 inches apart. Lay a pencil across them (use a pencil with flat sides so it won't roll).

3 Put the paper towel wing on the side of a ruler, lined up with the end of the ruler. Place the ruler and wing on the pencil so that it balances like a seesaw. The end of the wing and ruler should stretch over the edge of the table.

4 Hold a hair dryer, on cool setting, about 12 inches from the front of the wing. Blow the air onto the front of the wing. The air pressure will be lower above the wing as the air moves up and over it, and the seesaw balance will begin to tip. This tipping is the lift that helps to keep the aircraft up.

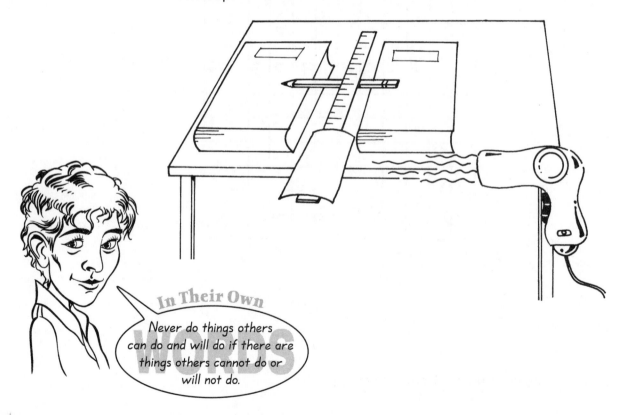

In Their Own WORDS

Never do things others can do and will do if there are things others cannot do or will not do.

CHARLES A. LINDBERGH

Born *February 4, 1902, Detroit, Michigan*
Died *August 26, 1974, Kipahulu, Maui, Hawaii*

The 1920s was called the "golden age" of airplane flight, as hundreds of courageous men and women risked their lives to fly farther, faster, and higher than anyone before. The contest that fascinated people the most was a $25,000 prize for the first nonstop flight from New York to Paris. Nearly all the great flyers of the day were eager to try, but the one who captured the prize, along with the admiration of millions, was a modest young pilot named Charles A. Lindbergh. His 33½ hour flight was hailed as one of the most heroic feats of the century.

The twenty-five-year-old Lindbergh had been bitten by the "flying bug" while a student at the University of Wisconsin. He dropped out of college to go to flying school and then trained with the army, becoming a captain in the U.S. Air Service in 1924. After a stint of "barnstorming" (touring the country performing stunts) and pioneering airmail service, he decided to try for the New York-to-Paris prize.

When Lindbergh showed up at a Long Island airstrip in a single-engine plane he had helped design, other aviators called him the "flying fool" for daring to try it alone. Nine others had already tried and failed; four had died, three had been injured, and two were missing. On a rainy morning in May 1927, Lindbergh was the only one to try to take off. His plane was so heavy with fuel that he barely cleared the telephone lines at the end of the runway.

For the next 33½ hours, Lindbergh's *Spirit of St. Louis* droned on across the stormy Atlantic Ocean. After 17 hours, he noted, "My back is stiff; my face burns. All I want is to throw myself down flat . . . and sleep." When he landed safely outside Paris, he was stunned to see a crowd of one hundred thousand people rushing to greet him. The shy, boyishly handsome Lindbergh was given a hero's welcome wherever he went. As a London newspaper put it, "His daring dazzles the world."

His 1929 marriage to Anne Morrow, daughter of a diplomat, only added to his fame. In 1932, the Lindberghs' infant son was kidnapped and murdered. To escape still more publicity, the couple quietly moved to England. Several trips to Nazi Germany convinced Lindbergh that the United States would be foolish to fight Nazi power. When he returned to the United States he caused outrage by becoming a leading *isolationist*, one who was opposed to U.S. involvement in World War II.

Removing Weight

"A plane that's got to break the world's record," Lindbergh said, "should be stripped of every ounce of weight." To do that, he flew without radio, lights, fuel gauges, and parachute, and without a copilot. When he took off, Lloyd's of London refused to quote odds on his chances of success, because "the risk is too great."

Heart Doctor

In the mid-1930s, Lindbergh worked with Dr. Alexis Carrel on experiments that helped Carrel develop the first artificial heart.

Things You'll Need

1 large sheet of white paper
scissors
string
ruler
transparent tape

When the Japanese attack on Pearl Harbor forced the United States into the war, Lindbergh supported the Allied cause with enthusiasm and secretly flew fifty combat missions against the Japanese. In 1954, President Eisenhower named him a brigadier general in the Air Force Reserve; he served as a consultant to the Department of Defense and to a commercial airline. He died in Hawaii in 1974.

Work Out the Numbers

1 Lindbergh completed the New York-to-Paris flight of 3,600 miles in 33 hours and 30 minutes. What was his average speed?

2 Before flying across the ocean, Lindbergh completed a cross-country flight from San Diego to Long Island in 21 hours, 20 minutes and averaged 140 mph. What is the distance from San Diego to Long Island?

Answers appear at the back of the book.

Testing Air Flow and Flight

Why is the tail of an airplane essential for flight? Find out in this experiment.

1 Cut a strip from the sheet of paper, 2 inches by 12 inches. Attach a 24-inch string to one end of the strip with tape. Hold the end of the string and swing the paper back and forth.

2 Now cut a second, more narrow strip—¼ inch by 12 inches. Attach it to the other end of the wider strip. Now swing the paper back and forth again. Notice the change. The second time you moved the strip, the movement of the paper was much smoother.

The paper moves forward at an angle, causing the air to flow faster over the top side. This exerts more uplift on the bottom of the strip. The angle of the paper keeps changing, so the pressure also changes, and these changes make the paper twist and turn wildly. Adding the paper tail makes the angle more constant, so the flow of air is smoother across the paper and there is less twisting.

In Their Own Words

It is the greatest shot of adrenaline to be doing what you have wanted to do so badly. You almost feel like you could fly without the plane.

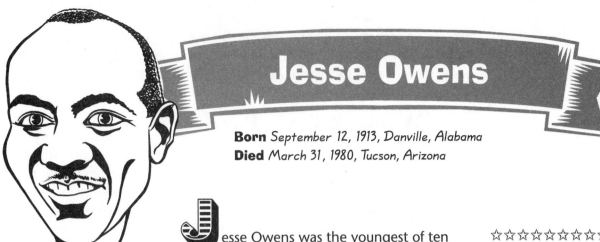

Jesse Owens

Born *September 12, 1913, Danville, Alabama*
Died *March 31, 1980, Tucson, Arizona*

Jesse Owens was the youngest of ten children born to a family of Alabama share-croppers. His name was James Cleveland Owens, but he seemed too small for such a big name, so he was called J. C. and then Jesse. Jesse was short and slightly built, but he had wings on his feet, and he would one day use that gift to carry a message from his people, and from all Americans, directly to Adolf Hitler, the dictator of Nazi Germany.

The Owens family joined the African American migration to the North in the 1920s, and Jesse developed his running and other track skills in Cleveland schools. He first gained nationwide attention in 1932 when he tied the world record in the 100-meter dash (10.4 seconds). The next year, at the National Interscholastic Championship in Chicago, he won the 100-yard dash, the long jump, and the low hurdles.

As a sophomore at Ohio State University in 1935, he stunned the nation by setting three world records and tying a fourth, all in one day. His records were in the 220-yard dash (20.3 seconds), the 220-yard low hurdles (22.6 seconds), and the running broad jump (26' 8¼"), and he tied the world record in the 100-yard dash (9.4 seconds). His broad jump record did not become official until after the 1936 Olympics.

Jesse Owens's greatest triumph came in the 1936 Olympic Games, held in Berlin. Hitler planned to use the games to showcase the superiority of the Aryan (Germanic) "race." Owens took care of that by winning four gold medals, tying the Olympic record in the 100-meter sprint (10.3 seconds), and then setting new Olympic and world records in the running broad jump (26' 5⁵⁄₁₅") and the 200-meter sprint (20.7 seconds) and running anchor on the winning 400-meter relay team. Hitler left the stadium rather than present gold medals to a black man. Jesse Owens later observed: "It dawned on me with blinding brightness. I realized: I had jumped into another rare kind of stratosphere—one that only a handful of people in every generation are lucky enough to know."

Owens decided to retire from track after that great achievement. He graduated from Ohio State in 1937 and, after an unsuccessful attempt at business, became secretary of the Illinois Athletic Commission, where he served until 1955. After a goodwill tour of India for the U.S. Department of State, he established the "junior sized Olympic Games" and promoted

☆☆☆☆☆☆☆☆☆☆☆
African American Patriots

Jesse Owens was not the only African American athlete to put a large hole in Adolf Hitler's notion of racial superiority. In 1938, two years after Owens's feat, African American boxer Joe Louis joined the cause when he crushed German heavyweight champion Max Schmeling in a second-round knock-out. (Although Schmeling was used by the Nazis, he himself refused to join the party or to abandon his Jewish friends. Joe Louis became Schmeling's friend, and Schmeling later gave money to Louis's widow.)

☆☆☆☆☆☆☆☆☆☆☆

other sports for young people. He was an excellent public speaker, constantly in demand for inspirational talks to business and government audiences. Owens died in Tucson, Arizona, in March 1980.

Winner's-Circle Puzzle

In this puzzle you have to figure out what letter in the winner's circle can be added to each group of four letters in the larger circle, which, when unscrambled, make six five-letter words related to the career of Jesse Owens. Remember that the letter in the winner's circle must stay the same.

Example: Suppose the 4 letters are *MJSP*, and you try *U* in the winner's circle. This gives you *MJSPU*, which unscrambles to *JUMPS*.

Answers appear at the back of the book.

Gold Medal Awards

Things You'll Need

2 cups flour
½ cup salt
2 tablespoons cream of tartar
measuring cups and spoons
saucepan
1 cup water
2 tablespoons cooking oil
adult helper
mixing spoon
waxed paper
rolling pin
round glass, about 4 inches in diameter
pencil or drinking straw
wire cooling rack
paintbrush
poster paints
red, blue, and white ribbon (about 22 inches of each color)

Make some Olympic-style medals out of clay with a long ribbon for placing the medal over the winner's head. Choose a contest, such as shooting baskets or running races. Have your friends compete, then have an award ceremony, with refreshments where you give the medals to the first-, second-, and third-place finishers.

1 To make a batch of clay, stir together the flour, salt, and cream of tartar in a saucepan. Stir in the water and cooking oil. With an adult's help, cook the mixture for 3 to 5 minutes over medium heat, stirring constantly.

2 Spoon the clay onto a sheet of waxed paper and let it cool a few minutes. Roll out the clay to a thickness of about ¼ inch. Press the glass into the clay to make three circular medals. Use a pencil or drinking straw to make a hole near the edge; the hole should be large enough for the ribbon to squeeze through.

3 Place the medals on a wire rack and let them harden for at least twelve hours. Paint one red, one blue, and one white. After the paint has dried, push the matching colored ribbon through the hole in each. Your awards are now ready for your medal ceremony.

In Their Own WORDS

It all goes so fast, and character makes the difference when it's close.

DOUGLAS ★★★★★★★★★★★★★★★★★★★★★★★★★

MACARTHUR

★★★★★★★★★★★★★★★★★★★★★★★★★★★★★★★★★★★★

Born *January 26, 1880, near Little Rock, Arkansas*
Died *April 5, 1964, Washington, D.C.*

Douglas MacArthur's entire life was devoted to the United States Army. He was born on an army base, the son of a general, and graduated at the top of his West Point class in 1903. During World War I (1914–1918) he first showed the military skill and independence that would mark his career. He organized the famous 42nd ("Rainbow") Division, became its commander, and was decorated for distinguished service. His confidence in his military judgment led to a brilliant career characterized by bold, creative moves. But that great confidence also caused trouble during the Korean War.

Between the wars (1919–1939), he served in various army posts, including superintendent of West Point (1919–1922) and army chief of staff (1930–1935). By 1941, when the United States entered World War II, MacArthur was commander of U.S. forces in the Far East.

MacArthur became one of the great heroes of that war. When Japanese forces overran American and Filipino defenders in the Philippines in 1942, President Roosevelt ordered MacArthur to escape to Australia to plan the Allied counteroffensive. As he left, he promised his troops, "I shall return." Thirty-six months later, he kept that famous promise by leading the American assault on Japan's Pacific empire. At the end of the war, MacArthur was given the honor of accepting Japan's surrender on the deck of the USS *Missouri* on September 2, 1945, and he was made a five-star general. As commander of the occupation of Japan, MacArthur performed brilliantly. Under his guidance, a disarmed Japan became a democracy.

The Korean War (1950–1953) brought MacArthur's career to an unusual end. When China's communist troops came to the aid of their North Korean ally, MacArthur, as supreme allied commander, asked for permission to bomb the Chinese bridges across the Yalu River. Fearing an escalation of the war, President Harry S. Truman refused that permission. When MacArthur publicly criticized the president, Truman dismissed him.

The Defeat of the Bonus Army

In 1932, during the Great Depression, several thousand World War I veterans built a shantytown in Washington, D.C., to petition the government to release their promised bonuses a few years early. Under orders from President Herbert Hoover, General MacArthur led army troops in destroying the shantytown and driving out the veterans. MacArthur was criticized for this move. So was his second-in-command, future president Dwight D. Eisenhower.

MacArthur returned home to a hero's welcome and received strong support from Truman's enemies in Congress. Somewhat reluctantly, Congress upheld the president's constitutional authority to dismiss a general. MacArthur soon retired to private life. He died in Washington, D.C., on April 5, 1964, at the age of eighty-four.

☆ ☆

A Golden Oldie

In 1951, after being dismissed by President Truman, MacArthur made a dramatic speech to a joint session of Congress. He concluded with the emotional statement that "Old soldiers never die, they just fade away." It turned out that the words were from a song that had been popular at the time of the Spanish-American War in 1898. Several popular singers rushed to record this old nugget, and it soon made it to the top ten.

☆ ☆

Invisible Writing

Things You'll Need

¼ to ½ cup of lemon juice (for variation, try milk, grapefruit juice, or baking powder dissolved in water)

small paper cup

cotton swab

1 sheet of paper

2 sheets scrap paper

electric iron and ironing board

adult helper

During World War II, the Japanese military had a very elaborate secret code, but American code experts managed to decipher it. The Japanese never believed that their code had been broken, but to be safe, they scrambled to make other codes. Here's a kind of code device that was used in 1944. You can try it, and you can also try one or two of the variations by changing ingredients.

1 Pour the lemon juice into the small paper cup. Use your thumbnail to scrape about half the cotton off one end of a cotton swab and twirl the end to make as sharp a point as possible. Dip the "pen" into the "invisible ink" and write a short, simple message, such as, "Enemy moving on left flank." (You have to write carefully because you won't be able to see the letters as you write.)

2 Place the message sheet between two pieces of scrap paper on an ironing board. With the help of an adult, set the iron to warm, then iron the papers with the warm iron.

Your message will instantly emerge. Try other invisible inks, too.

Miniature Japanese Sand Garden

General MacArthur spent many years in Asia and became a great admirer of the culture of China, Korea, the Philippines, and Japan. As commander of the occupation forces in Japan, he became particularly fond of the miniature sand gardens, called Zen gardens. The idea was to create a tiny corner of nature that you could enjoy in quiet contemplation.

Make your own version of a sand garden and create a quiet space for yourself and your thoughts.

1 Fill the box nearly to the top with sand, and use the ruler to make the surface smooth. Space the stones, pebbles, and moss randomly, some in clusters, others alone; some on top of the sand, some partly buried. Use the comb to make wavelike swirls in the sand.

2 Experiment slowly with different arrangements. Try to let the garden arrange itself. Spend some time enjoying this miniature quiet space.

© 2006 by John Wiley & Sons, Inc.

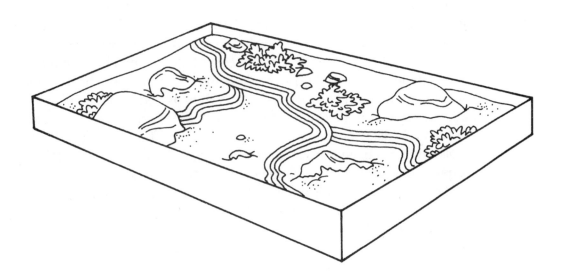

Things You'll Need

gift box with shallow sides, about 12 inches by 20 inches (or a shoebox)

1 or 2 pails of clean sand (available at hardware stores)

6-inch ruler

5 or 6 stones of different shapes and sizes

4 or 5 small pebbles

3 or 4 pieces of dried moss

old pocket comb

In Their Own **WORDS**

We are not retreating— we are advancing in another direction.

Rachel Carson

Born May 27, 1907, Springdale, Pennsylvania
Died April 16, 1964, Silver Spring, Maryland

When Rachel Carson was growing up in a small Pennsylvania town, she was eager to pursue a career as a writer. Later, as a student at the Pennsylvania College for Women (now Chatham College), she encountered an outstanding professor who inspired her to switch her major from English to biology. That was a good choice, because she soon found a way to combine her love of writing with her devotion to science.

Another powerful influence on her career was summer work at the Marine Biological Laboratory in Woods Hole, Massachusetts. Those summers filled her with wonder about life in the sea and led to her fame as an author. Her first book, *Under the Sea Wind* (1941), combined her scientific analysis with an elegant writing style. Over the next ten years, she wrote a variety of pamphlets and articles on conservation as part of her work as an aquatic biologist with the United States Bureau of Fisheries (later renamed the Fish and Wildlife Service). In 1951, she published *The Sea Around Us*, a best seller that has been translated into more than thirty languages. The book gave her worldwide fame and financial independence. Four years later, *The Edge of the Sea* was published, another award-winning best seller.

Carson's last book, *Silent Spring* (1962), was the slender volume that rocked the world. The book opened with a fable about a future year when spring came to a silent land: "On the mornings that had once throbbed with the dawn chorus of robins, catbirds, doves, jays, wrens, and other bird voices, there was now no sound; only silence lay over the fields and woods and marsh." Carson said that the fable would come true unless people stopped using deadly chemicals, such as DDT, to kill weeds and insects. Carson explained how the poison was carried through the food chain to larger animals.

People throughout the nation and the world responded to her warning. By 1970, Americans were organizing the first Earth Day—a celebration of the new awareness. In 1972, Congress banned the use of DDT and created the Environmental Protection Agency (EPA). Rachel Carson did not live to see the results of her pioneering work. She died in Silver Spring, Maryland, on April 16, 1964. A newspaper editorial summed up her contribution: "A few thousand words from her, and the world took a new direction."

An Early Start

Like several of the heroes in this book, Rachel Carson got off to an early start. When she was eleven years old, one of her stories was published in a children's magazine.

A Rachel Carson Tribute

In 1970, the Bureau of Sport Fisheries and Wildlife established the Rachel Carson National Wildlife Refuge in Maine. A plaque at the entrance contains a quotation in which she summarized her work:

"All the life of the planet is interrelated. . . . Each species has its own ties to others, and . . . all are related to the earth. This is the theme of *The Sea Around Us*, and the other sea books, and it is the message of *Silent Spring*."

How Pollution Spreads

Rachel Carson noted that after chemicals were sprayed on crops, a residue of the poisons spread to new plantings and even to neighboring fields. One way the chemicals spread was through capillary action— the movement of liquid through the tiny cells in plant fiber. Here are some experiments to demonstrate this action.

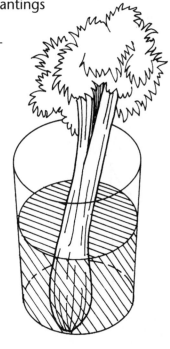

Things You'll Need

small glass
water
food coloring
1 stalk celery
4 small bowls or cups
white string, about 10 inches

1 Fill a small glass with water about halfway. Add a few drops of food coloring. Stand a stalk of celery in the glass and watch the color move up the stalk. In the same way, chemicals that have leached into the soil or into groundwater will move up the roots of a plant.

2 Fill the four bowls or cups with water, nearly to the top, and add different-color food coloring to each. Dip the end of the string into one bowl, then drape it over the edge and into the second bowl. Stretch the string through the water in the second bowl, then on into the third and fourth. In a few minutes you'll be able to watch the colored water crawl along the string out of each bowl.

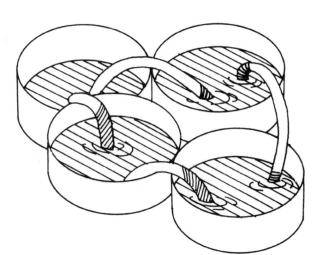

★ Finding Leaf Colors

★ Things You'll Need

about ¼ cup of sand
plastic bowl
3 or 4 green leaves
adult helper
disposable gloves
about ½ cup rubbing alcohol
smooth rock
glass jar (with wide mouth)
piece of paper
2 paper clips

One of Carson's greatest pleasures was in helping young children explore the natural world. If a child asked where the autumn colors in leaves come from, she might demonstrate that the colors are already in the leaf, but they are hidden by the green. You can find out how this works in this experiment.

1 Place the sand in the bowl and add the leaves. With the adult's help, add enough alcohol to cover the leaves. (Wear disposable gloves to avoid mild skin irritation.)

2 Use the rock to crush the leaves into tiny pieces. The sand will help pulverize the leaf material. You'll see the alcohol turn green as it pulls the pigment out of the leaves.

3 Carefully pour the green alcohol into a glass jar. Discard the sand. Roll a piece of paper into a cylinder. Hold the ends together with a paper clip. Place the paper cylinder in the jar and set it out of the way overnight. By morning, you will see that the pigments have crawled up the paper. Because the pigments move at different speeds, the different colors will separate from one another, revealing the colors hidden in the leaf.

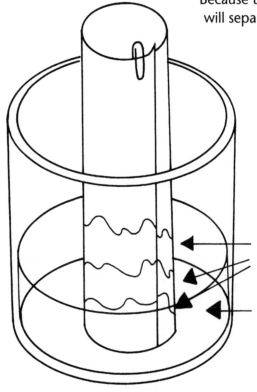

different
color lines

alcohol

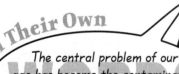

In Their Own WORDS

The central problem of our age has become the contamination of man's total environment with . . . substances of incredible potential for harm.

ROSA PARKS

Born *February 4, 1913, Tuskegee, Alabama*
Died *October 24, 2005, Detroit, Michigan*

One of the most dramatic events of the twentieth century began quietly on December 1, 1955, when a Montgomery, Alabama, bus driver ordered a seamstress named Rosa Parks to give up her seat to a white man. She refused. Police were called, and Parks was arrested and ordered to pay a fine. That incident turned out to be the spark that ignited the civil rights movement.

Born in Tuskegee, Alabama, in 1913, Rosa grew up with the *discrimination* (differentiation on the basis of color) and *segregation* (separation) that made African Americans second-class citizens. She had attended a school where there were no white children, and she was used to signs on drinking fountains, theater balconies, and train stations that read "FOR COLORED ONLY."

About the time Rosa married a barber named Raymond Parks, she came to know African Americans, and some white people, who believed change was possible. She began to do volunteer work for the National Association for the Advancement of Colored People (NAACP). In 1955, she agreed to defy segregation on the Montgomery, Alabama, city buses so that the NAACP could take her case to court. Her lawyers claimed that the segregation deprived her of her basic constitutional rights.

While the Rosa Parks legal case made its way through the courts, the African American people of Montgomery followed the inspired leadership of a young minister, the Reverend Martin Luther King Jr., and began to *boycott* (refuse to use) the city buses. Week after week, empty buses rattled through the streets of Montgomery's African American neighborhoods. Parks and others braved the threats and violence of white segregationists.

After 382 days, the Montgomery bus boycott ended when the United States Supreme Court ruled that segregated seating on city buses was unconstitutional. It was a huge victory for African Americans and for the idea of peaceful, or nonviolent, resistance to racial discrimination. For her brave act, Rosa Parks became known as the "mother of the civil rights movement."

The Montgomery Bus Boycott

The African American population of Montgomery supported the bus boycott by walking and by forming car pools with more than three hundred drivers, including a number of white housewives who avoided arrest by saying they were driving their housekeepers. Leaders of the white segregationists tried threats and arrests to stop them. When insurance companies canceled the drivers' car insurance, people bought insurance from Lloyd's of London.

93

Rosa Parks lost her job because of her protest. After the bus boycott, she moved to Detroit, where she continued to work for the civil rights movement. She also worked for Congressman John Conyers of Michigan from 1965 to 1988, and in 1987 she founded the Rosa and Raymond Parks Institute for Self-Development, promoting educational goals for young people.

The Highest Award

In 1999, Rosa Parks was awarded the Congressional Medal of Honor, the highest award the nation can give a civilian.

★ A Rosa Parks Word Search

Hidden in the puzzle below are an even dozen words associated with Rosa Parks and the Montgomery bus boycott. Can you find them all? The letters can go across, from left to right or right to left, up or down, or on the diagonal.

RIGHTS	LAW	MARCH	EQUAL
BUS	BOYCOTT	MINISTER	SEAT
RIDER	COURT	ROSA	ARREST

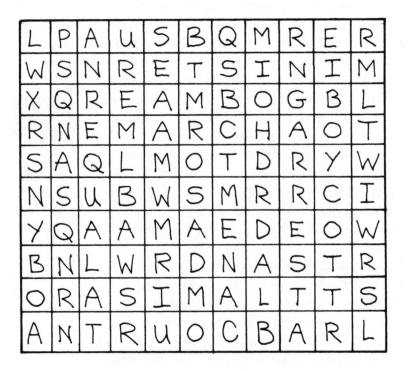

L	P	A	U	S	B	Q	M	R	E	R
W	S	N	R	E	T	S	I	N	I	M
X	Q	R	E	A	M	B	O	G	B	L
R	N	E	M	A	R	C	H	A	O	T
S	A	Q	L	M	O	T	D	R	Y	W
N	S	U	B	W	S	M	R	R	C	I
Y	Q	A	A	M	A	E	D	E	O	W
B	N	L	W	R	D	N	A	S	T	R
O	R	A	S	I	M	A	L	T	T	S
A	N	T	R	U	O	C	B	A	R	L

Answers appear at the back of the book.

Drawing a Neighborhood Map

The Montgomery bus boycott required extraordinary planning and dedication. Precise routes had to be planned for every car pool. Drivers and substitutes had to be ready for every assignment. One step in the planning process was the creation of maps to guide car poolers through different neighborhoods.

To get a feeling for what was involved—and have some fun in the process—try drawing a map of your neighborhood or part of it.

Things You'll Need

ruler
car odometer (with an adult's help)
compass (optional)
pencil
3 or 4 sheets of white paper
colored pencils or crayons

1 First, choose the area you want to map. A park would be good, or a neighborhood block, even a school bus route.

2 If possible, measure distances for accuracy, either by pacing it off and estimating, or, for longer distances, by car (with Mom or Dad driving, of course!). Use a compass to find north if you don't know where north is. Make a rough sketch as you go, including symbols to represent objects, such as houses, trees, and roads.

3 Draw a legend for your map, including a title, the symbols, and a scale of distances, such as 1 inch = 100 feet, or ½ inch = 1 mile.

4 Transfer your sketch neatly onto a clean sheet of paper to make a final version. Add color and your map legend.

In Their Own WORDS

I would like to be known as a person who is concerned about freedom and equality and justice and prosperity for all people.

JOHN F. KENNEDY

Born *May 29, 1917, Hyannis, Massachusetts*
Died *November 22, 1963, Dallas, Texas*

The presidency of John Fitzgerald Kennedy lasted less than three years, but in that time he led the country with such intelligence, grace, and compassion that his administration became known as "Camelot," after the mythical English kingdom of King Arthur.

Kennedy was born into a large, wealthy Catholic family in which the males were steered toward careers in politics and public service. In spite of nagging health problems, John completed his college education at Harvard in 1940. He wrote his senior thesis about the failure of England to prevent the rebuilding of Germany's military by Nazi dictator Adolf Hitler. Published as *Why England Slept* in 1940, the year he graduated, the book became a best seller.

Kennedy served heroically in the navy during World War II (1941–1945). While he was commander of a PT boat in the South Pacific, a Japanese ship rammed his boat, cutting it in two. In spite of injuries, Kennedy guided his surviving crew members to safety, swimming for four hours and saving an injured crewman by towing him by pulling on his life jacket strap with his teeth. He was elected to the House of Representatives in 1946 and was reelected twice, and then won a Senate seat in 1952. Even while recovering from two spinal surgeries, he advanced his career by writing *Profiles in Courage*, published in 1956, a best-selling book that also won a Pulitzer Prize.

In the 1960 presidential election, Kennedy won a narrow victory over Richard Nixon to become the youngest man elected to that office and the first Roman Catholic. Kennedy gave the country a new kind of presidency. He and his wife, Jacqueline ("Jackie"), were young, attractive, intelligent, and idealistic, filling the White House with a lively zest for art and culture. Many of Kennedy's programs won strong popular support, especially the Peace Corps, which sent thousands of Americans to poor regions of the world to help people help themselves. He was also praised for his handling of the Cuban Missile Crisis in October 1962, a showdown with the Soviet Union in which the president averted what could have become a nuclear war. In addition, he challenged the nation's space program to "safely land a man on the moon by the end of the decade"—a project that won great public support and ultimately succeeded.

Robert Kennedy

John's brother Robert once climbed a fourteen-thousand-foot mountain in the Yukon, one of the highest peaks in North America. He left there three tie clips commemorating John's World War II PT boat, plus a copy of John's inaugural address. One thing that made the feat so remarkable was that Robert was afraid of heights!

In November 1963, the Kennedys were riding in a Dallas motorcade when JFK was shot and killed, apparently by a lone assassin, Lee Harvey Oswald. His tragic death added to the image of the nearly ideal president. In a speech he had planned to deliver in Dallas, Kennedy wrote, "It should be clear by now that a nation can be no stronger abroad than it is at home. Only an America which practices what it preaches about equal rights and social justice will be respected."

☆ ☆

The Political Kennedys

Two of President Kennedy's brothers achieved political prominence. Robert Kennedy (1925–1968) served as his brother's attorney general and became a champion of civil rights. He was elected senator from New York State in 1964 and became a leading candidate for the 1968 Democratic presidential nomination. Like his brother, Robert was shot and killed by a lone assassin, Jordanian-born Sirhan Sirhan. Ted Kennedy, the youngest of the Kennedy children, was elected senator from Massachusetts in 1962, filling John's term, and then was reelected seven more times, most recently in 2000. Several younger Kennedys have also been active in politics and public service.

☆ ☆

Double Chocolate Brownies

President Kennedy said that he was fond of any kind of dessert, as long as it was chocolate! This popular 1960s recipe would have been one of his favorites.

1 Preheat oven to 350 degrees F.

2 Have an adult help you melt the butter and chocolate in the top of a double boiler or in a microwavable bowl. Allow the mixture to cool.

3 Break the eggs into a mixing bowl and beat them well. Stir in the sugar, then add the cooled chocolate mixture.

4 Sift the flour into the mixture, add the vanilla, and blend thoroughly.

5 Pour into a greased 8-by-8-inch pan, and bake at 350 degrees for 25 to 35 minutes.

6 *To make frosting:* Melt the chocolate in a double boiler or microwavable bowl. Remove. Add butter, sugar, and cream. Blend in the vanilla.

7 Use oven mitts to remove the pan, and frost the brownies while they are still hot.

adult helper
½ cup butter
3 squares chocolate
double boiler or microwavable bowl
2 eggs, well beaten
mixing bowl
egg beater or blender
wooden mixing spoon
1 cup sugar
½ cup flour
1 teaspoon vanilla extract
sifter
greased 8-by-8-inch pan
oven mitts
table knife or spatula

Frosting:
1 square chocolate
1 tablespoon butter
1 cup confectioner's sugar
1 teaspoon cream
½ teaspoon vanilla extract
MAKES 16 BROWNIES

Keep Track of Your Exercise Progress

Things **You'll Need**

paper
pencil
ruler

President Kennedy exercised rigorously every day, to stay in shape and also as a way of dealing with constant back pain. He swam every day in a pool heated to 90 degrees and also completed 25 minutes of exercises.

To build yourself up to a regular routine, keep a chart of your progress for two or three weeks until you reach your goals, then keep it going. Begin by going over your goals with a parent or your school physical education instructor. With help from your school librarian, find the current recommendations of the President's Council on Physical Fitness, a program promoted by President Kennedy.

1 Use pencil and ruler to divide the paper into fourteen columns to cover 2 weeks. List your first exercise, such as jumping jacks, and do five the first two or three days. Then add five more for two or three days, and continue until you reach a goal of, say, twenty-five jumping jacks every day.

2 Add a second exercise, such as touching your toes, and follow the same procedure.

3 Continue with a third, fourth, and fifth exercise.

4 Review your plan with the adult advising you, and decide on ways to make it an ongoing program.

In Their Own WORDS

Let every nation know, whether it wishes us well or ill, that we shall pay any price, bear any burden, meet any hardship, support any friend, oppose any foe to assure the survival and the success of liberty.

98

Jackie Robinson

Born *January 31, 1919, Cairo, Georgia*
Died *October 24, 1972, Stamford, Connecticut*

On April 11, 1947, history was made at Brooklyn's Ebbets Field when Jackie Robinson trotted out to his position at second base for the Brooklyn Dodgers—the first African American to play major league baseball.

Robinson needed enormous courage to challenge baseball's color line, and Branch Rickey, the president of the Brooklyn Dodgers, chose wisely when he selected Robinson for this task. Born in Georgia in 1919, Robinson grew up in California, where he became an outstanding athlete in baseball, football, track, and basketball. He starred in all four sports in high school and college. In 1945, after serving three years in the army during World War II, he played baseball for the Kansas City Monarchs in the Negro National League, and that led to the phone call from Rickey.

The Dodger owner warned Robinson that he would face abuse and danger, and the ballplayer assured Rickey that he could take it. "But, Mr. Rickey," Robinson asked, "do you want a player who's afraid to fight back?" Rickey said, "I want a player with guts enough *not* to fight back." From the first day, Robinson endured jeers and taunts from fans and other players. Ugly threats were made on his life. Opposing pitchers threw at his head, and base runners came into second base with their spikes high. He could not eat with his teammates or stay in the same hotel, even in Northern cities.

Robinson endured the abuse with remarkable dignity. He also quickly made it clear that he was one of the most skilled and exciting players in the game. He was named Rookie of the Year in 1947. In 1949 he led the league in batting and was named Most Valuable Player. Within two years the jeers turned to cheers. Robinson's spectacular success led other teams to sign African American players, and other professional sports began to hire them, too.

Robinson and other players also began to urge baseball clubs to use their economic power to force hotels and restaurants to

The Negro Leagues

Until Robinson's dramatic breaking of the "color barrier" in baseball, African Americans played in the Negro Leagues—professional teams that included many outstanding players who surely would have been stars in major league baseball. After Robinson's success, several players, including the famous pitcher Sachel Paige, who was in his forties by the time he could sign a major league contract, moved from the Negro Leagues to the Majors.

Stealing Home

One of the most exciting moments in baseball—and one of the rarest—is when a base runner steals home. No one was better at this feat than Jackie Robinson. Baseball writers and fans said that the peak of suspense came in a few games between the Dodgers and the New York Giants when Robinson stood on third base and Sal Maglie was pitching for the archrival Giants. In one of those games, in 1949, the game was scoreless going into the ninth inning. Robinson hit a double, stole third, and then headed for home as Maglie pitched. Robinson slid under the tag to score the only run of the game.

© 2006 by John Wiley & Sons, Inc.

integrate—to serve people of all racial and ethnic backgrounds. After retiring from baseball in 1956, he became a business executive and served on several community boards. He continued to push for increased opportunities for African Americans. Two weeks after being honored at the opening of the 1972 World Series, Robinson died suddenly in Stamford, Connecticut.

Work Out the Numbers

Baseball players and fans live by statistics, and batting average is one of the most important—how many hits a player has in how many times at bat. Batting average is figured by dividing the number of at bats into the number of hits. If a player has 4 at bats and manages 2 hits, his average is .500.

1 In 1947, Jackie Robinson had 175 hits in 590 at bats. His average for the year was _____.

2 Robinson won the batting title in 1949, with 203 hits in 593 times at bat. His batting average for the year was _____.

3 Over the course of his ten-year major league career, Robinson came to bat 4,877 times and had 1,518 hits. His lifetime average was _____.

Answers appear at the back of the book.

Testing the Curveball

Things You'll Need

string—about 30 inches long
masking tape or packaging tape
golf ball
table
yardstick

One of the hardest pitches for a batter to hit is the curveball. The ball curves in one direction from a right-handed pitcher and in the opposite direction from a lefty. Try this experiment to measure the curve of a ball. As you'll see, the secret is in making the ball spin.

1 Attach one end of the string to the ball and the other to the top edge of the table. Make sure the attachments are firm and the ball will swing freely.

2 Place the yardstick on the floor directly under the path where the ball will be swinging.

3 Hold the ball and twist the string forty to fifty times in a counterclockwise direction. Pull the ball back as far as it will go (without loosening the tape) and let it go.

4 Let the ball swing back and forth. Use the yardstick on the floor to help you observe how the ball curves as it swings.

The ball is moving in two directions: while moving forward, it is also spinning on its axis. This causes the air to flow around the ball in two different directions. As the pitcher throws the ball forward, the spin he puts on it will cause the ball to swerve (or curve) to one side as it goes forward. What happens if you twist the string in a clockwise direction?

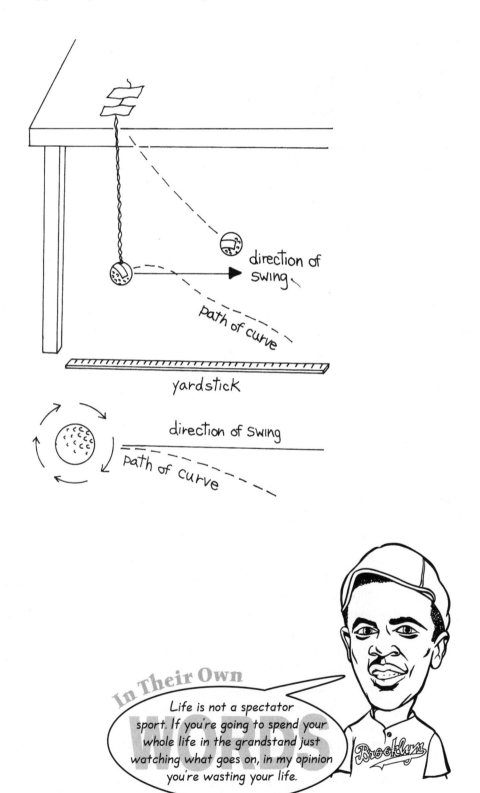

In Their Own **WORDS**

Life is not a spectator sport. If you're going to spend your whole life in the grandstand just watching what goes on, in my opinion you're wasting your life.

Betty Friedan

Born *February 4, 1921, Peoria, Illinois*

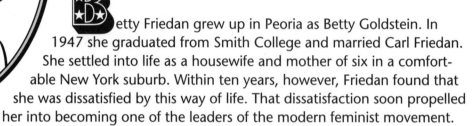

Betty Friedan grew up in Peoria as Betty Goldstein. In 1947 she graduated from Smith College and married Carl Friedan. She settled into life as a housewife and mother of six in a comfortable New York suburb. Within ten years, however, Friedan found that she was dissatisfied by this way of life. That dissatisfaction soon propelled her into becoming one of the leaders of the modern feminist movement.

The change in her life began quietly in 1957 when she sent a questionnaire to her college classmates to see if they shared her feelings. The response was overwhelming, with the great majority expressing despair with their roles as suburban housewives and mothers. "Each suburban wife struggled with it alone," Friedan wrote. "As she made the beds, shopped for groceries, she was afraid to ask even of herself the silent question—'Is this all?'" She made a careful study of the subject, which she published in 1963 as a book titled *The Feminine Mystique*.

The Feminine Mystique was an instant best seller. Friedan's generation, she said, growing up in the Depression and World War II (1941–1945), was "vulnerable, lonely, frightened [with] a pent-up hunger for marriage, home, and children." Too late, they found their lives to be hollow and empty. Women throughout the country responded to Friedan's book. A new feminist movement swept the country as women began demanding the chance for opportunities outside the home.

In 1966, Friedan became the major founder of NOW (the National Organization for Women), and served as its president until 1970. Under her leadership, NOW pressed for greater career and job opportunities for women. She also worked for legalized abortion and for the Equal Rights Amendment (ERA). In addition, she urged women to join a 1970 protest march, which feminists called a nationwide strike, to publicize their demands on the fiftieth anniversary of women's gaining the right to vote.

After years of turmoil, including a divorce from her husband in 1969, Friedan modified her views. In a 1981 book, *The Second Stage*, she argued that women did not have to choose either career or family, that it was possible to work outside the home *and* enjoy the comfort and love of marriage and children.

☆☆☆☆☆☆☆☆☆☆☆

Symbolic Changes

While Friedan, and NOW, often worked for major changes, like legalization of abortion, she also pressured for smaller changes that had symbolic significance. For example, the Help Wanted columns in newspapers traditionally separated ads into jobs "For Men" and "For Women." Friedan played a major role in having the gender distinction removed.

☆☆☆☆☆☆☆☆☆☆☆

Strike Slogan

During the 1970 strike, NOW's slogan for women was a takeoff on the advice to "strike while the iron is hot." The new slogan was: "Don't iron while the strike is hot."

Word Search

Here's a word search, with twelve words associated with Betty Friedan. The words can go up or down, forward or backward, or diagonally.

strike	women	family	work
NOW	rights	equal	home
feminist	amendment	ERA	children

S	Q	R	L	R	I	G	H	T	S	N
N	O	K	M	E	R	A	S	Q	T	D
W	O	R	K	L	N	L	C	N	R	W
W	B	O	L	A	U	Q	E	R	I	H
R	N	W	G	F	E	M	O	H	K	Y
C	E	M	O	H	D	A	R	R	E	L
H	K	E	S	N	A	B	C	L	M	I
F	I	F	E	M	I	N	I	S	T	M
W	O	M	E	N	A	Q	M	H	H	A
N	A	N	E	R	D	L	I	H	C	F

Answers appear at the back of the book.

Photo Album

Betty Friedan started her second career by contacting her classmates from college. You can keep track of your school friends with photographs, collecting the pictures in albums like the one you'll make in this project. In keeping with Friedan's model, ask your friends to write their opinion about a question or issue that is important to all of you.

1 Use the ruler and pencil to measure a piece of wrapping paper about 6 by 8 inches. Cut it out and place it face down on your work surface. Position one piece of the cardboard on it and cut off the four corners, as shown in the drawing.

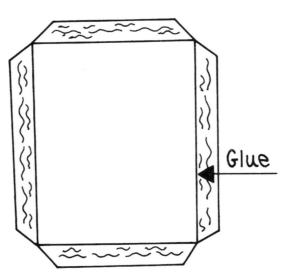

Glue

Things You'll Need

ruler
pencil
gift wrapping paper, 1 or 2 sheets, in lively patterns
scissors
2 pieces of stiff cardboard, 5 by 7 inches
craft or white glue
felt-tip pen or marker, any color
paper cutter
heavy white paper
hole punch
short piece of yarn
photo mounts (or photo cement)
photos

103

2 Put thin ribbons of glue on the back of the wrapping paper. Fold the four flaps over and glue them to the cardboard. This will be the front cover of your book. Repeat with the other piece of cardboard to make a back cover.

3 Use the felt-tip pen to write a title and your name on the cover. (If the pattern on the paper is too dense for the writing, use a self-adhesive label for your name and title.)

4 Use the paper cutter or scissors to cut fifteen to twenty sheets of heavy white paper down to 5 by 7 inches.

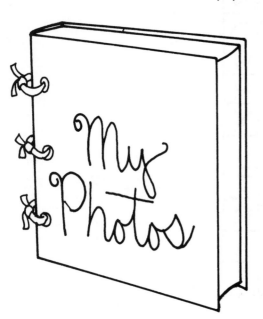

5 On the front cover, make marks for three holes. The holes should be ¾ inch from the left edge. Mark holes 1 inch from the top, 1 inch from the bottom, and in the middle (about 2½ inches from top or bottom). Use the hole punch to make the three holes.

6 Use this cover as a template to make three matching holes in the back cover and in all the white sheets.

7 Place the sheets inside the covers and run pieces of yarn through the holes. Tie the yarn in square knots. Your album is ready to use. Photos can be put in with photo mounts or photo adhesive. Add more sheets when necessary, or make another album.

In Their Own WORDS

Man is not the enemy here, but the fellow victim.

CESAR ★★★★★★★★★★★★★★★★★★★★★★★★★★★★★

CHAVEZ
★★★★★★★★★★★★★★★★★★★★★★★★★★★★★★★★★★

Born *March 31, 1927, near Yuma, Arizona*
Died *April 13, 1993, San Luis, Arizona*

Cesar Chavez was born into a family of migrant farm workers in 1927 near Yuma, Arizona. He grew up in the hard years of the Great Depression, working with his parents as a farm laborer, moving from one migrant camp to another, wherever crops were ready to harvest. He became determined to change conditions for the farm workers who worked ten to twelve hours a day, six days a week, and lived in camps that were unsanitary and without any comforts. The work was back-breaking, with low wages, no benefits, and little chance for children to go to school.

In 1952, Chavez joined a new community organization, the Community Service Organization (CSO). He rose to be director of CSO but resigned in 1962 to try to organize farm workers into a union. He slowly built the National Farm Workers Association (NFWA) into a strong union in the interior farm valleys of California.

In 1965, he led a strike against the grape growers around Delano. With support from other unions, the workers held their own through the long strike. Chavez used the techniques of the civil rights movement, insisting on nonviolence. In 1968, Chavez called for a nationwide boycott of California grapes. While many people thought the boycott was bound to fail, consumers throughout the country supported the effort, which became known as "*La Causa*" ("The Cause"). Finally, in July 1970—five years after the strike began—grape growers gave in and accepted the union, now called the United Farm Workers (UFW).

Chavez thought legislation was needed to protect workers' rights, and while he helped make sure the California Agriculture Labor Relations Act was passed, government indifference meant little real change. In 1984, when growers refused to control the use of pesticides, which were harmful to the workers'

Better Schooling

When Chavez was growing up, his family had to move so often that by the eighth grade he had attended nearly forty different schools. He never did go to high school. One of his first projects with the Community Service Organization was to get the workers' children into schools.

Chavez and Nonviolence

Chavez used a variety of techniques that were common to the civil rights movement. In addition to pickets, strikes, union organizing, and community meetings, he led a protest march to Sacramento, the California state capital, in 1966 that created nationwide support for the workers' demands. Two years later, Chavez went on a hunger strike, a technique used effectively by Mahatma Gandhi in India. For several weeks he refused to eat. His determination kept public attention on his cause—stopping the violence used against workers. This technique was also successful in building sympathy and support for the movement.

health, he launched another boycott. Once again, the growers yielded to union pressure.

For thirty years, Chavez worked without letup to help some of the country's poorest workers achieve better wages and improved working conditions. He died in San Luis, Arizona, on April 13, 1993.

★ Build a Word

Use the clues to figure out each of the words associated with Cesar Chavez. The letters inside the squares will form a seventh word, which is scrambled. Unscramble it to find another Chavez-related word.

1 A technique used by labor unions.

1 ☐ _ _ _ _ _

2 Part of the name of his union.

2 _ _ _ _ ☐ _

3 They opposed the union's demands.

3 ☐ _ _ _ _ _ _

4 Workers lived in migrant _____.

4 _ _ _ ☐ _

5 A farm worker who moves often.

5 _ _ _ ☐ _ _ _

6 Where a migrant harvests crops.

6 _ ☐ _ _

7 What the Delano strike involved.

7 _ _ _ _ _ _ _

Answers appear at the back of the book.

★ Pinole

Things You'll **Need**

measuring cup
1 cup cornmeal
cookie sheet
adult helper
⅓ cup sugar
½ teaspoon cinnamon
¼ teaspoon ground nutmeg
saucepan
large spoon
3 cups milk

Because they were poor, migrant farm workers had to make basic foods stretch as far as possible. A standard warm breakfast or anytime meal was *pinole* (pronounced pi-NO-lee).

1 Spread the cornmeal on a cookie sheet. Bake at 425 degrees for 5 minutes, stirring two or three times. Make sure an adult helps you with the oven and stove.

2 Remove the cornmeal and let it cool, while you mix together the sugar, cinnamon, and nutmeg.

3 Pour the cornmeal into a saucepan. Add the sugar-and-spice mixture. Stir well.

4 Stir in the milk, a little at a time, stirring constantly. Cook over medium heat and continue stirring for about 15 minutes, or until the pinole thickens. Allow to cool for a few minutes before serving.

In Their Own WORDS

Even more important than money is a thing called dignity or self-respect or honor.

MARTIN LUTHER KING JR.

Born *January 15, 1929, Atlanta, Georgia*
Died *April 4, 1968, Memphis, Tennessee*

Martin Luther King Jr. was born in Atlanta in 1929, the son of a minister. Encouraged by his father, King got off to an early start in his education, skipping several grades in school and entering Morehouse College in 1944, when he was fifteen. He was ordained a minister at age eighteen, and he was twenty-six when he became pastor of Montgomery's Dexter Avenue Baptist Church in 1955. He soon emerged as a major leader of the civil rights movement, combining courage, an eloquent speaking style, and an unflinching commitment to nonviolence.

King learned about nonviolent protest during his college and graduate school years, by studying the life and teachings of India's Mahatma Gandhi. Gandhi had used nonviolent techniques, also known as passive resistance, to force Great Britain to grant India its independence.

Soon after becoming pastor in Montgomery, King was chosen to lead the Montgomery bus boycott. King electrified the city's African Americans with stirring speeches and demonstrated how to achieve change without violence.

Over the twelve years that followed the successful bus boycott, King led civil rights activists to some spectacular victories over racial segregation and discrimination. In 1957, the Southern Christian Leadership Conference (SCLC) was formed, with King as its president, determined to broaden the desegregation movement throughout the South.

King led the effort to get African Americans to register to vote. Voter registration campaigns in Selma and Montgomery, Alabama, and in Albany, Georgia, gained attention throughout the nation and the world

☆ ☆

"I Have a Dream"

King's August 1963 speech is his most famous for its eloquent challenge to the nation to achieve the ideal set forth by Thomas Jefferson in the Declaration of Independence that "all men are created equal." He personalized the dream by relating it to his four young children. Here is an excerpt from King's speech:

> I have a dream that one day this nation will rise up and live out the true meaning of its creed: "We hold these truths to be self-evident: that all men are created equal.". . . I have a dream that my four little children will one day live in a nation where they will not be judged by the color of their skin but by the content of their character.

☆ ☆

Letter from the Birmingham Jail

In 1963, when King was arrested and jailed in Birmingham, a group of ministers wrote a letter criticizing King for his aggressive tactics and suggesting that a more moderate approach might bring better results. Furious, King wrote an open letter in response, saying that those in power never granted rights of their own volition. African Americans, he argued, would not gain equality until they demanded it. King was in solitary confinement at the time, so he wrote the letter in the margins of a newspaper and had his lawyer smuggle it out of the prison.

when television news cameras showed peaceful protest marchers being confronted by police armed with clubs and attack dogs. King himself was beaten, stoned, and jailed, and his house was firebombed. His career reached a dramatic climax in August 1963, when he led the huge March on Washington and delivered his famous "I Have a Dream" speech from the steps of the Lincoln Memorial. He was awarded the Nobel Peace Prize a year later.

Early in 1968, King was in Memphis to support city workers, mostly African Americans, who were involved in a bitter strike. On April 4, 1968, he was assassinated by a sniper, James Earl Ray.

In 1986, King's birthday—January 15—was made a federal holiday. His widow, Coretta Scott King, continues to work for the cause.

★ Word Choices

Fill in the blanks with one of the words listed here.

> segregation   boycott   discrimination

1 Refusing to serve customers in a restaurant because they are African American would be a case of _____.

2 A theater that admitted blacks but only if they sat in the balcony was guilty of _____.

3 Refusing to eat in a restaurant that denied service to African Americans is called a _____.

Answers appear at the back of the book.

In Their Own WORDS

Injustice anywhere is a threat to justice everywhere.

NEIL ARMSTRONG

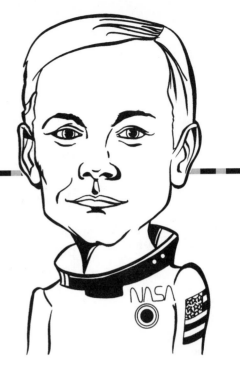

Born *August 5, 1930, near Wapakoneta, Ohio*

Neil Armstrong, future astronaut, had lofty ambitions from an early age. He dreamed about flying while he made model airplanes in the small town in Ohio where he grew up in the 1930s and early 1940s. He learned to fly as a teenager and earned his pilot's license on his sixteenth birthday. At the age of seventeen he entered Purdue University as a naval air cadet.

Called to active duty during the Korean War (1950–1953), Armstrong flew seventy-eight combat missions and was awarded the Air Medal three times. After the war, he became a test pilot and then, in 1962, was accepted into the new astronaut training program of NASA (the National Aeronautics and Space Administration). The space program had become a competition between the United States and the Soviet Union as the two superpowers vied to be the first to land a man on the Moon and return him safely.

Armstrong's first space flight, in 1966, was a dramatic one. He was performing the first-ever docking maneuver, connecting the spacecraft to a target vehicle. After a successful docking, his spacecraft, *Gemini 8*, suddenly began spinning wildly. Armstrong remained calm, brought the spacecraft under control, and returned safely to Earth.

On July 16, 1969, millions of people throughout the world stared in wonder at their TV sets as spaceship *Apollo 11*, commanded by Armstrong, with astronauts Edwin "Buzz" Aldrin and Michael Collins, sped half a million miles from Earth to the Moon. Four days later, Armstrong steered the spaceship's landing module—*Eagle*—to a soft landing on the edge of the Moon's Sea of Tranquillity. "The *Eagle* has landed," Armstrong announced dramatically as television cameras beamed the event back to Earth.

Armstrong then climbed down a ladder and became the first human to set foot on the Moon—a great triumph for the American space program and one of the most exciting moments of the century. "That's one small step for a man," Armstrong said, "and one giant leap for mankind." Armstrong and Aldrin then toured the Moon surface near their landing point, collecting soil and rock samples and taking pictures.

☆☆☆☆☆☆☆☆☆☆☆

Faster Than a Speeding Bullet!

Armstrong's favorite experimental plane was the *Bell S-15* rocket plane. It reached an altitude of sixty-seven miles and a top speed of 4,534 mph—twice the speed of a rifle bullet!

☆☆☆☆☆☆☆☆☆☆☆

Wanted: Civilian Astronaut

At the time of the Moon landing, the country was sharply divided over the Vietnam War. NASA officials, urged by the White House, decided that Armstrong was the better choice for the honor of being the first human on the Moon because he was a civilian. Buzz Aldrin, who many thought would be chosen, was still a colonel in the Air Force. In addition, Armstrong's calm action in the near-disaster with *Gemini 8* made him a natural choice.

Armstrong made no more space flights and retired from the astronaut corps in 1970 and spent a year as a NASA administrator. He also served as chairman of the Peace Corps National Advisory Council and became a consultant to several corporations. In 1971, he became a professor at the University of Cincinnati. Now retired, he lives on his small dairy farm in rural Ohio.

★ Testing Jet Propulsion

★ Things **You'll Need**

piece of cardboard, about 1 by 5 inches

scissors

transparent tape

15 to 20 feet of strong thread or fishing line

drinking straw

balloon (the long, sausage-shape balloons work best)

Jet propulsion is different from motor power. A jet airplane achieves its power by thrusting a jet of energy out of the tail, and this thrust pushes the craft in the opposite direction—or forward. Modern rockets and space-craft achieve liftoff in the same way. Here's a simple test to demonstrate how jet propulsion works.

1 To make the wings for your jet craft, round the ends of the cardboard. Cut a small V in the center of the wings to hold the straw in place while you tape, as shown in the drawing.

2 Use narrow strips of tape to attach the wings to the straw, about 2 inches from one end of the straw.

3 Run the thread through the straw. Tie one end of the thread to the back of a chair (or any suitable object) and the other end to another chair. Adjust the chairs to make the line as taut as possible.

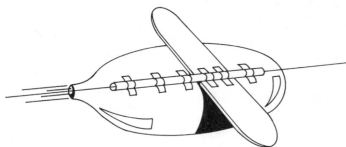

4 Have three or four pieces of tape ready. Blow up the balloon. Hold the neck closed with one hand and tape the balloon to the straw with your other hand. You might want to have a helper assist you.

5 As soon as the tape is applied, release the balloon and watch the jet of air propel your craft across the room.

★ Things **You'll Need**

several sheets of newspaper

flour

water

2 bowls—one low, rather flat bowl

wax paper

transparent tape

more sheets of newspaper

modeling clay

flat stick or clay modeling tool

toothpick

★ Model Moonscape

The *Apollo 11* Moon landing gave people on Earth vast amounts of information about what the surface of the Moon is like. It also corrected some misconceptions. For example, there had been some fear that the astronauts might land in soft "moon dust," several feet deep. There was no moon dust.

Use your own papier-mâché and clay model of a moonscape to show some of the Moon's features.

1 Spread newspaper on your work surface and mix a batch of papier-mâché: Mix flour and water into a sticky paste. Continue mixing until the paste is smooth but not watery.

2 Tape wax paper on the bottom of the shallow bowl to protect it. Apply papier-mâché by tearing newspaper sheets into strips about 1 inch wide by 5 or 6 inches long. Dip the strips in the paste and apply them to the protected bowl. Apply a layer of strips in a crisscross pattern and allow it to dry for 2 or 3 days.

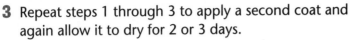

3 Repeat steps 1 through 3 to apply a second coat and again allow it to dry for 2 or 3 days.

4 When the model is dry, cover the surface with a thin layer of modeling clay. Use a flat stick, modeling tools, and a toothpick to form some of the Moon's features.

Some of the most common features are listed here.

Marias: These "lunar seas" are not seas but large, dark plains.

Craters: Rounded areas with circular walls where the surface was hit by meteors. Some craters are thousands of miles deep and thousands of miles across.

Rays: Bright streaks that extend out from some craters.

Rills: Long, narrow trenches that look like rivers from Earth. Some are several hundred miles long.

Domes: Small mounds that look like sand dunes.

Scarps: These are cliffs; some are thousands of feet high.

In Their Own WORDS

That's one small step for a man, one giant leap for mankind.

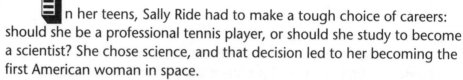

Sally Ride

Born *May 26, 1959, Los Angeles, California*

In her teens, Sally Ride had to make a tough choice of careers: should she be a professional tennis player, or should she study to become a scientist? She chose science, and that decision led to her becoming the first American woman in space.

Sally Ride was born in Los Angeles in 1959, the daughter of teachers who encouraged her tendency to be different from other girls. In neighborhood football and baseball games, Sally was often the first player chosen, and usually the only girl. In her teens, she became one of the best junior tennis players in the country, and there was a strong temptation to turn pro. But she also loved science. For a college, she chose Stanford University, one of the leading schools for science *and* for tennis. By the time she graduated with a degree in physics, she was committed to a science career and did graduate work in astronomy at UCLA.

In 1978, Ride was one of five women out of eight thousand people with science training to apply for the astronaut program of NASA (National Aeronautics and Space Administration). She completed the rigorous training to become a mission specialist, conducting experiments in space. The training included tests of mental and physical toughness as well as learning to maneuver in a weightless state.

On June 18, 1983, Sally Ride made history when she rode the space shuttle *Challenger* into Earth orbit—the first American woman in space. She operated the shuttle's 50-foot-long mechanical arm, which she had helped to design. She used the arm to place two communications satellites in orbit.

Ride returned to a hero's welcome and became a national celebrity, although she did her best to avoid the spotlight. She returned to space the following year in another *Challenger* mission. She left NASA in 1987 to teach—first at Stanford, then at the University of California at San Diego, where she was also director of the California Space Institute. Dr. Ride devotes much of her time to encouraging girls to explore science careers. The Sally Ride Science Festival, held in California every summer, is an exciting chance for girls in grades 5 through 8 to learn about their future career opportunities.

A Russian First

A Russian *cosmonaut* (the Russian word for astronaut), Valentina Tereshkova, orbited Earth in 1963 to become the first woman in space, twenty years before Sally Ride.

Space Fashions

The spacesuits worn by the first generation of astronauts were monster affairs, made of twenty-one layers and weighing 183 pounds. When Sally Ride and a few other women joined the program, they found one item missing: there were no pajamas (for when they were in orbit and could shed the weighty spacesuits). In the past, the all-male crews had simply slept in undershorts and T-shirts. When Ride and fellow astronaut Kathryn Sullivan pointed out the omission, NASA designers quickly corrected the problem.

Measuring Earth's Rotation

In using *Challenger's* mechanical arm to launch communications satellites, astronaut Ride had to consider the influence of Earth's rotation. This would enable her to chart the best time to place the satellite in orbit. You can make a simple measurement of Earth's rotation in your home.

1 Ask an adult to help you push the nail through the ball to make a hole. Remove the nail, and push a knitting needle all the way through the hole so that about an inch of the sharp end shows.

2 Tie the end of the kite string to the other end of the needle. The ball, needle, and string form a pendulum.

3 Tape the other end of the string to the ceiling. The needle should come within a few inches off the floor, but make sure that it can swing freely.

4 With ruler and pen, draw a straight line on the sheet of paper. Tape the paper to the floor underneath the pendulum. Start the pendulum swinging so that the back-and-forth movement follows the line.

5 Wait an hour or two and see what happens. The pendulum should still swing in its original arc, but it will no longer follow the black line because of Earth's rotation.

Note: At the United Nations building in New York, a large pendulum is constantly swinging to demonstrate Earth's rotation in the same way.

© 2006 by John Wiley & Sons, Inc.

Things You'll Need

adult helper
long nail
small rubber ball (4 or 5 inches in diameter)
knitting needle
kite string, fishing line, or any strong string, 8 to 10 feet long
transparent tape
ruler
black felt-tip pen
sheet of white paper

Space Scramble

Each of the nine scrambled words on the left has something to do with Sally Ride's *Challenger* mission. Write the unscrambled words in the boxes. The first one is done for you. Read down the column of boxes to find a tenth space-mission word.

APSEC   S P A C E

INSCCEE

BRIOT

THREA

SISINOM

EACHMNCALI

ANSA

TTUHSEL

LISATETEL

In Their Own WORDS

I didn't come into the space program to be the first woman in space. I came to get a chance to fly as soon as I could.

113

Maya★Lin

Born *October 5, 1959, Athens, Ohio*

In 1980, when Maya Lin was a college student studying architecture, she read about a competition to design a memorial honoring Americans killed in Vietnam. She decided to enter, seeing it as a chance to help heal the nation's wounds after the bitter divisions created by that war. Because she was young and lacked experience, she was stunned to learn she had won the competition over more than 1,400 entrants.

Born in Athens, Ohio, in 1959, Maya Lin grew up in a home filled with books and art. Her parents, who had left China during the communist takeover of 1949, were professors at Ohio University. Her mother taught literature, and her father taught art. Lin enjoyed learning in both Eastern and Western traditions—the East's emphasis on philosophy and religion, the West's strength in practical fields like science and math.

Lin received her B.A. degree in architecture from Yale University in 1981 and a master's degree in 1986. When the Vietnam Memorial she designed was dedicated in 1982 in Washington, D.C., she was disappointed in the lukewarm response of the public. She had purposely avoided creating a towering heroic monument. Instead, she wanted to emphasize ordinary human beings who had died in the tragedy. But the long, low wall containing the names of every American killed in the war did not fit people's idea of a heroic monument.

But as people began to experience the wall, something happened. The memorial began to affect visitors. Family members and friends searched for names. They left letters, notes, flowers, and mementos. "The Wall," as people now called it, was having a healing effect. Today, more than one million visitors come to the memorial every year, making it the most visited work of contemporary art in the United States.

Since that great success, Maya Lin has been very busy and constantly in demand, working as a combination architect, designer, and sculptor. Her designs often unite made objects with elements of nature. In one of her most famous works, for example, the Civil Rights Memorial (1988–1993) in Montgomery, Alabama, visitors read words and names through a thin sheet of running water flowing over polished stone.

Lin has won numerous awards and now works from her own design studio in New York City. She lives in New York with her husband, Daniel Wolf, and their two children.

Helping the Environment

Maya Lin is deeply concerned about protecting the environment and constantly looks for ways that she as an artist can help. One project, which she began in 2004, involves working with the Natural Resources Defense Council to design a paper recycling center for New York City.

More Awards

Lin has also won awards for building design, including the Museum for African Art (1984–1992) in the SoHo section of New York City and the Langston Hughes Library (1999) in Clinton, Tennessee.

Mobile Sculpture

Maya Lin likes to combine nature with art, and you can have fun doing the same thing in this sculpture project. First, make a collection of small natural items you find outdoors in your neighborhood—twigs, a leaf, a feather, a stone, a blossom; or you might focus your search on beach items (shells, coral, dried seaweed) or things around the house (small toys or parts of them, or kitchen items).

Things You'll Need

collection of 8 to 10 found objects

4 or 5 branches and twigs, different lengths

strong black thread or fishing line

1 Spread out the collected objects on your work surface.

2 For your main cross-piece, use a fairly thick branch, 12 to 14 inches long.

3 Experiment with two or three smaller branches as smaller cross-pieces. Use short pieces of thread to attach some of your objects to the cross-pieces, as shown in the drawing. The key to a mobile is to keep everything in balance. Keep arranging and rearranging until you have a mobile that is both pleasing and balanced.

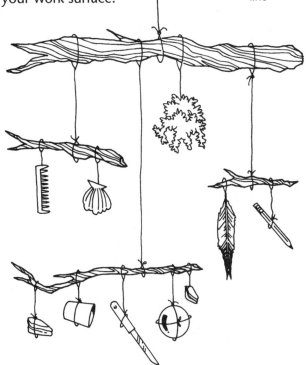

Design a Memorial

Imagine there is a contest to design a memorial for a recent event. Choose an event that honors rescuers and others, such as those who helped people in the terrible tsunami that swept through Indonesia and across the Indian Ocean in December 2004 or the attack on the World Trade Center in September 2001.

Plan your memorial as a statue, building, fountain, or some other structure that would be put in a public place. Decide what your theme will be, what materials should be used, and what kind of legend or dedication you want to include. Think about how people can interact with the memorial, as they do with Maya Lin's work.

Make several sketches of what the memorial will look like, then make a finished drawing that includes the legend or dedication.

In Their Own WORDS

It terrifed me to have an idea of mine to be no longer a part of my mind, but totally public.

NSWERS

Paul Revere

A B C D E F G H I J K L M N O P Q R S T U V W X Y Z
Z Y X W V U T S R Q P O N M L K J I H G F E D C B A

THE REGIMENT WILL MARCH AT DAWN

Patrick Henry

1. **T** R E A S O N
2. L I B E **R** T Y
3. L A W Y E **R**
4. C **O** N G R E S S
5. D E **A** T H
6. C O N C O **R** D
7. T R R O A O = ORATOR

Thomas Jefferson

READ WITH CARE

Sequoyah
Building Words

1. BARN
2. BARGE
3. BARK
4. BARBER
5. BARGAIN
6. BARBECUE
7. BARBED WIRE
8. BARTER
9. BARBARIAN
10. BAROMETER
11. BARITONE
12. BARTENDER

Measuring the Trail of Tears

1. About 600 miles
2. Tennessee, North Carolina, Georgia, and Alabama
3. Iowa, Sauk, Fox, Potawatomi, Chippewa, Kickapoo, Seneca, Shawnee, Ottawa, Choctaw, Chickasaw, Creek, and Seminole
4. Seminole, Seneca, Shawnee, and Ottawa

Abraham Lincoln

1. P E A **C** E
2. B A **T** T L E
3. P R **O** C L A M A T I O N
4. U N **I** O N
5. S L A **V** E R Y
6. F **R** E E D O M
7. C O N F E D E R A C **Y**
8. C T O I V R Y = VICTORY

Harriet Tubman

Here are some of the words in the honeycomb.

REAP	SHAPE
HERO	SHINE
SHIN	YEARN
YEAR	TROVE
PLOT	SHEER
VETO	SHALE
LEAP	SHOVE
ROTE	SHORT
VERY	SHORE
NEAR	STOVE
PEAR	SHOVEL
PLAY	REPLAY
LORE	SHIVER
THREE	SHINY
ROLE	

Susan B. Anthony

England 1918

Switzerland 1971

France 1944

United States 1920

New Zealand 1893

Wyoming 1869

Ulysses S. Grant

1. 47 days × 2,500 shells = 117,500

2. Union: 43 percent
    Confederate: 27.5 percent

3. Union: about 125,000
    Confederate: about 67,000

Sitting Bull

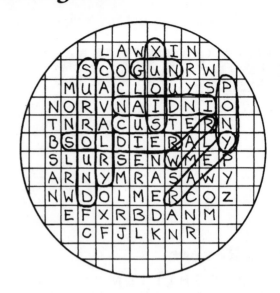

Alexander Graham Bell

THE END DOES NOT JUSTIFY THE MEANS.

Booker T. Washington

1. S L **A** V E R Y

2. E **D** U C A T E

3. T H E M S E **L** V E S

4. **R** I G H T S

5. R A C **E**

6. S E G R **E** G A T I O N

7. A D L R E E = LEADER

Oliver Wendell Holmes Jr.

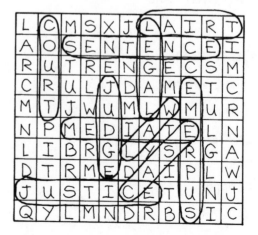

118

Jane Addams

1. C H I C A G O   D
2. S L U M   S
3. H U L L   D
4. C O U R T   A
5. R E F O R M   M
6. C H I L D   L A B O R   N
7. R E S I D E N T   A
8. C I T Y   E
9. H O U S E   J
10. P E A C E   A

     Answer: JANE ADDAMS

W. E. B. Du Bois

A) O U T
B) S H E L F
C) F L O C K
D) B L O C K S
E) B A C K

Quotation: "THE SOULS OF BLACK FOLK"

Albert Einstein

     Mystery letter: E

1. TIME
2. CELL
3. TUBE
4. HEAT
5. LENS
6. WAVE

Franklin D. Roosevelt

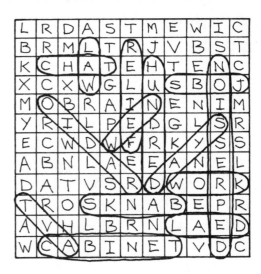

Frances Perkins

1. PRAC**T**ICES
2. CABIN**E**T
3. FA**I**R
4. LABO**R**
5. **U**NIONS
6. **S**ECRETARY
7. **C**ONGRESS
8. EMPLO**Y**MENT

Answer: T E I R U S C Y = SECURITY

Amelia Earhart

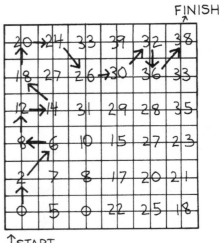

Charles A. Lindbergh

1. 107.5 mph
2. 2,987 miles

Jesse Owens

The letter in the Winner's Circle is "E"

FIELD

RELAY   MEDAL

E

GAMES   TEAMS

LEADS

Rosa Parks

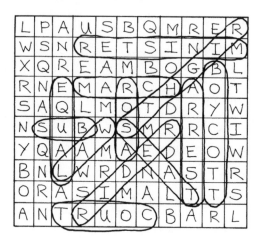

Jackie Robinson

1. .297
2. .342
3. .311

Betty Friedan

Cesar Chavez

1. **S** T R I K E
2. U N I T **E** D
3. **G** R O W E R S
4. C A M P **S**
5. M I G **R** A N T
6. F A **R** M
7. S E G P R A = GRAPES

Martin Luther King Jr.

1. discrimination
2. segregation
3. boycott

Sally Ride

S P **A** C E
S C I E N C E
O R B I **T**
E A **R** T H
M I S S I **O** N
M E C H A **N** I C A L
N **A** S A
S H **U** T T L E
S A **T** E L L I T E

NDEX